The Good Robot

ALSO AVAILABLE FROM BLOOMSBURY

Philosophical Posthumanism, Francesca Ferrando
Exceptional Technologies, Dominic Smith
Günther Anders' Philosophy of Technology, Babette Babich
Posthuman Glossary, Rosi Braidotti and Maria Hlavajova

The Good Robot

Why Technology Needs Feminism

Eleanor Drage and Kerry McInerney

BLOOMSBURY ACADEMIC
LONDON • NEW YORK • OXFORD • NEW DELHI • SYDNEY

BLOOMSBURY ACADEMIC
Bloomsbury Publishing Plc
50 Bedford Square, London, WC1B 3DP, UK
1385 Broadway, New York, NY 10018, USA
29 Earlsfort Terrace, Dublin 2, Ireland

BLOOMSBURY, BLOOMSBURY ACADEMIC and the Diana logo are trademarks of
Bloomsbury Publishing Plc

First published in Great Britain 2024

Copyright © Eleanor Drage and Kerry McInerney, and Contributors, 2024

Eleanor Drage and Kerry McInerney have asserted their right under the Copyright,
Designs and Patents Act, 1988, to be identified as Author of this work.

For legal purposes the Acknowledgments on p. ix constitute an extension of this
copyright page.

Cover illustration by Sinjin Li
Cover design by Ben Anslow

All rights reserved. No part of this publication may be reproduced or transmitted
in any form or by any means, electronic or mechanical, including photocopying, recording,
or any information storage or retrieval system, without prior permission in writing
from the publishers.

Bloomsbury Publishing Plc does not have any control over, or responsibility for, any third-
party websites referred to or in this book. All internet addresses given in this book were
correct at the time of going to press. The author and publisher regret any inconvenience
caused if addresses have changed or sites have ceased to exist, but can accept no
responsibility for any such changes.

A catalogue record for this book is available from the British Library.

A catalog record for this book is available from the Library of Congress.

ISBN: HB: 978-1-3503-9996-9
PB: 978-1-3503-9995-2
ePDF: 978-1-3503-9997-6
eBook: 978-1-3503-9998-3

Typeset by Deanta Global Publishing Services, Chennai, India
Printed and bound in Great Britain

To find out more about our authors and books visit www.bloomsbury.com and
sign up for our newsletters.

To what's possible

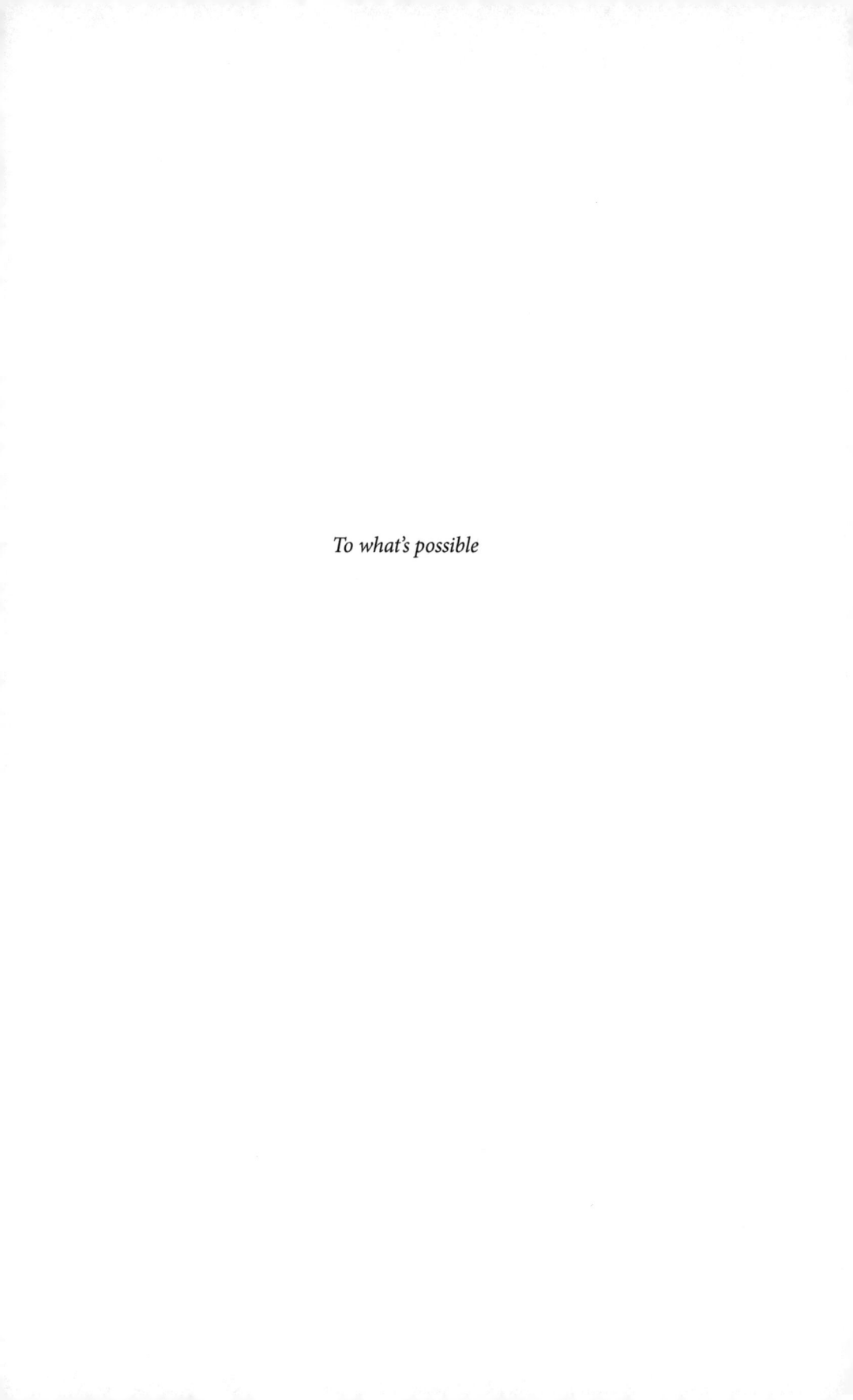

Contents

Acknowledgments ix

Introduction: Good Technology Is Feminist *Eleanor Drage and Kerry McInerney* 1

Part I Good Relations *Eleanor Drage* 11

1. Good Technology Is Cooperative *Blaise Agüera y Arcas* 13
2. Good Technology Is Messy *Jason Edward Lewis* 21
3. Good Technology Is Biophilic *N. Katherine Hayles* 28
4. Good Technology Is Earthly *Rosi Braidotti* 36
5. Good Technology Is Intergenerational *Sneha Revanur* 43

Part II Good Systems *Kerry McInerney* 51

6. Good Technology Is Inclusive *Margaret Mitchell* 55
7. Good Technology Is Possible—But There Are Conditions *Soraj Hongladarom* 64
8. Good Technology Is Community-Centric *Jennifer Lee* 71
9. Good Technology Is Participatory *David Adelani* 81

Part III Good Design *Kerry McInerney* 89

10. Good Technology Is Vulnerable *Os Keyes* 93
11. Good Technology Is Slow (to Scale) *Ranjit Singh* 100
12. Good Technology Is Accessible, Not Just "Good Enough" *Meryl Alper* 108

13 Good Technology Needs an Emergency Exit Door
    Priya Goswami 117
14 Good Technology Invites Response *hannah holtzclaw and
    Wendy Hui Kyong Chun* 125

Part IV Good Visions *Eleanor Drage* 133

15 Good Technology Is a Portal to Other Worlds *Felicity Amaya
    Schaeffer and Neda Atanasoski* 135
16 Good Technology Is/Not Asian Women *Anne Anlin Cheng* 145
17 Good Technology Holds Up a Mirror to Ourselves
    Michele Elam 153
18 Good Technology Needs Good Stories *Kanta Dihal* 160

Part V Good Rebellions *Eleanor Drage* 169

19 Good Technology Challenges Power *Catherine D'Ignazio* 171
20 Good Technology Is Free (At Least for a Moment)
    Frances Negrón-Muntaner 179
21 Good Technology Subverts Militarism *Katherine Chandler* 187
22 Good Technology Is a Fantasy *Jack Halberstam* 196

List of Contributors 203
Index 206

Acknowledgments

We would like to extend our thanks first and foremost to the generous funder of the Gender and Technology Project at the University of Cambridge Centre for Gender Studies, Christina Gaw. We met and started The Good Robot podcast as part of the wider Gender and Technology Project, and are incredibly grateful to Christina for funding and driving this work. We would also like to thank Christina for providing the funding for the volume's beautiful cover artwork and illustrations, created by Sinjin Li. Thank you also to our Principal Investigator on the Gender and Technology Project, Professor Jude Browne, for her leadership on the project.

Many thanks to our editorial team, the designers, and the production team at Bloomsbury Academic for capturing our vision and creating a book that we are truly proud to bring into the world. We would also like to thank Professor Rosi Braidotti for agreeing to host our book in her *Theory in the New Humanities*. Rosi was an early supporter of The Good Robot podcast, and her support has made all the difference.

This book would not have been possible without the care and support of so many incredible feminist thinkers, activists, technologists, and scholars. We are so grateful to everyone who has been part of our Good Robot community over the past two years, from our podcasts guests through to our support team at the University of Cambridge Centre for Gender Studies and the Leverhulme Centre for the Future of Intelligence.

Finally, thank you to all of our friends and family who have faithfully listened to the podcast and supported us in various ways over the past two years—from DEEPYCUB, who provided us with our theme music, to William McInerney, who provided us with extensive support and critique as we conceptualized and launched the podcast. We treasure you all.

Introduction: Good Technology Is Feminist

Eleanor Drage and Kerry McInerney

Technology needs feminism. Too often, conversations about feminism and technology are limited to the representation of women in science, technology, engineering, and mathematics (STEM). Alternatively, they fixate on the emergence of sex robots and other erotic technologies, the coverage of which is saturated by the intermingling of disgust and fetishistic pleasure. However, sexism, misogyny, and patriarchy are deeply interwoven throughout the tech industry and the products that we use on a daily basis. This includes the female-gendered voice assistants that are expected to answer our every beck and call; the various forms of tracking technologies from AirTags to Find My Phone, which are increasingly used for non-consensual surveillance and are facilitating coercive control and intimate partner violence; and the development of algorithms that claim to be able to deduce someone's sexuality from their facial appearance. New technologies often serve as a crucible for existing forms of injustice and oppression, albeit repackaged in a new, electronic form.

Meanwhile, technology has profoundly changed how we think and talk about feminism and the issues that lie at the heart of feminist activism and thought. We now frequently hear that men and women are biologically "programmed" to act and live in different ways, or "wired" up to recreate the same tired gender hierarchies and oppressive social structures. Instead of dieting, Silicon Valley bros inform us that our bodies can be "hacked"—in a nefarious new diet trend known as "biohacking"—for maximum health and productivity. And, in an era of virulent and overt transphobia—often in the erroneous name of feminism—we face calls to return to the simplistic thinking of binary code: two genders, 1 and 0. Amid all these technological metaphors, we sometimes lose sight of a greater truth: that despite all of this, feminism is *electric*. Feminist ideas, activism, and thought run like a golden current across generations. Feminism vibrantly illuminates the injustices of the world around us and galvanizes us to change them. Innately wild, it can be shocking, spiky, uncomfortable, and even dangerous. Most importantly, feminism is transformative, whether this takes the form of the immediate flash of a lightning bolt or the slow, steady burn of generational change. And that transformation is desperately needed. We need better *relations*, better *systems*, better *designs*, better *visions*, and perhaps, when these fail, better *rebellions*.

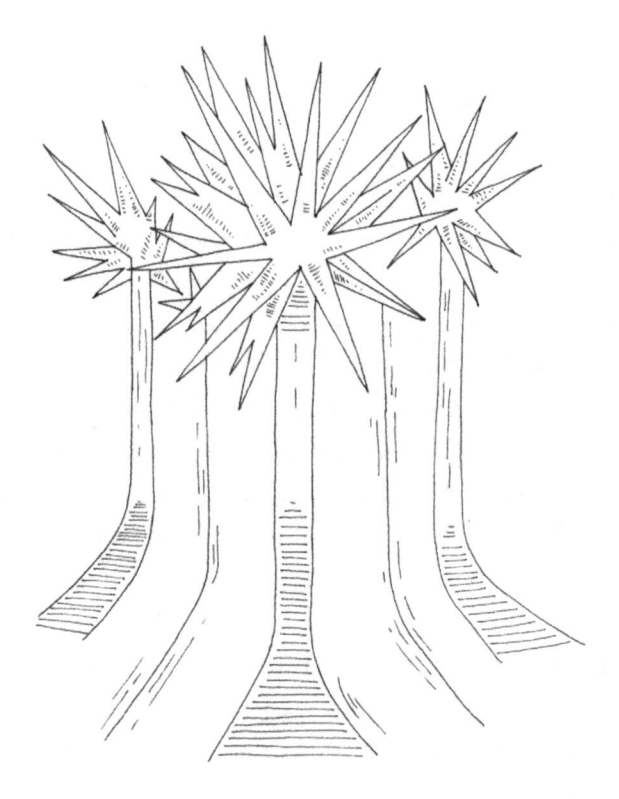

Provocation
Feminism is transformative, whether this takes the form of the immediate flash of a lightning bolt or the slow steady burn of generational change.

Calling for better technology is relatively uncontroversial. Calling for *good* technology, though, raises a whole host of political, ethical, social, and technological questions. In our day jobs, we work with tech companies to consider how feminist ethics and principles can be integrated into tech development. In this context, good technology might mean something as simple as a technology that functions as it is supposed to: technology that "works." Good technology, in industry contexts, is often reduced down to questions of functionality and errors. But our combined two decades-worth of interest in queer, feminist, anti-racist and decolonial thinking has led us to approach the question of "good technology" quite differently. Just because a technology functions as intended without any technical errors does not mean that it is designed with good intentions in mind, nor that it will be deployed in ways that more broadly support good outcomes for everyone. As historian of artificial intelligence (AI) Jonnie Penn emphasizes, good technology is often not really about technology at all but about other good things, like living well together, economic justice, and the redistribution of power. All our hype and preconceptions about technology may even be distractions in imagining good technology. Do we compromise on "good" when it is followed by the word "technology"?

Instead, we turn to gender, queer, and anti-racist studies, which when boiled down are about creating a world where everyone can live life well, even though inequality and persecution foreclose this possibility for many. As Judith Butler has pointed out, the aspiration to live a "good life" has led to profiting off the labor of others, which perpetuates inequality in global economic systems. To this we might add, developing technologies that put people who are already marginalized at risk of further violence and degradation. When she accepted the Adorno Prize in 2012, Butler said: "If we rely on ordinary language to tell us what the good life is, we will become confused, since the phrase has become a vector for competing schemes of value." This is why the vast majority of people in this book define and critique the idea of "good" in order to make its value-ladenness visible. Unlike science fiction writer Isaac Asimov, we do not approach technology ethics as a way of creating doctrine ("what are the rules of good tech?") but as a way to reorient technology toward serving the people who are most disenfranchised today. In other words, our goal is that every piece of technology is built in pursuit of justice. In what can seem like the unrelenting misery of our present era, filling our world with technologies that redistribute power puts a good future back on the horizon.

We know this is possible because of the people in this book. We are often told that you should not meet your heroes, lest you face the inevitable disappointment of realizing that they are just human, after all. So when we started *The Good Robot* podcast, we reached out to people with no small amount of trepidation. Would our heroes accept the invitation to be on our fledgling "feminism and technology" podcast? Would enough people identify as feminist, and would they want to chat to two young AI ethics researchers? Or would they turn us down and consign our dreams to the dustbin? As this book shows, the stars of technology, ethics, feminism, and philosophy proved the proverb wrong. While we fiddled away with our new microphones and scrambled to resolve technical errors, the leading thinkers in social justice and technology patiently chatted to us about their lives and work. Yes, they are all just human, but in their humanness they demonstrate the ethical ways of making, thinking about, and living with technology that they preach.

When we chose *The Good Robot* as the name for our podcast, we thought it might come across as flippant or idealistic. We liked its pithy invocation of kitsch, but we were worried that people might take it literally as the desire to create a "good robot." Instead, we have been pleasantly surprised by how academics and practitioners alike have responded to it as a provocation rather than a possibility. For them and for us, good robots are not utopian pipe dreams but prompts for thinking differently about the technology industry as it stands today. What was apparent at the end of the first season was that the idea of the good robot conjures something in everyone's mind, no matter how differently that prompt is interpreted. The good robot crosses disciplines, ages, and other borders, appealing to both technical and nontechnical audiences. We were delighted when in our interview with Jack Halberstam, he said, "I like this title, *The Good Robot*, because it's such a fantasy from an earlier moment that has not really come to pass." While it signals an unfulfillable and even outdated aspiration, our mascot still offers a moment of reflection about whether the good technologies that were hoped for have come about, whether good technology is too capacious (too large, too undefined, too roomy, too "wibbly") a term, and what more exacting definitions are required in order to bring about a better world.

Feminist Ethics
Slowness, vulnerability, magic, anger.

And so, it prompts our three key questions: What is good technology? Is it even possible? And, how can feminism help us get there? In some episodes we call these our "billion dollar questions," though with the helpful nudging of our interviewees we realized that we were letting these questions fall into the capitalist logic we were looking to circumvent. Priceless questions, then. You might ask why we are aiming for technology that is merely "good," as opposed to exploring the kinds of technology that could lead to social justice, or sustainable futures, or equality. But these ideas are implicit in our invocation of good technology, because as you would expect from critical thinkers—interviewees rarely take good at face value, and most often respond to "what is good tech?" by breaking down what "good" means. What good? And good for whom? Or, "Who's getting that good done to them and may not think it's very good?" as Catherine D'Ignazio and Lauren Klein ask in *Data Feminism*. This volume shows the breadth of answers that these cliched questions succeed in inviting, from good technology being free to good technology having an exit door. Coming up with answers is no easy feat; as with most things, it's easier to think about what we don't want from technology than what we do (hence our cinemas are full of technological dystopias rather than utopian scenarios). The good tech prompt challenges some of our brightest minds to consolidate their ideas into a list of priorities and offer us a roadmap for achieving them.

In these chapters, the people who make and study technology take that one step further by clearly communicating their most brilliant ideas to us, the people who use these technologies and experience their effects. While academic and technical work is often inaccessible to a wider audience, we wanted this collection to make you feel at home in the presence of rising and established stars. Indeed, this is true to the podcast's origins: we recorded our first episodes in the second lockdown of 2020, when everybody—even those who were "somebody"—were forced to stay inside. The cancellation of work, conferences, and lectures may have given us a leg up in having our invitations accepted by previously busy people now reckoning with a bare social calendar. This also meant interviewing the most eminent philosophers, activists, and tech practitioners from their bedrooms and kitchens, a thrill and a coziness that will be one of the only things we'll miss from the Covid-19 era. These chapters have been designed for people who are both very familiar with their work and those who have never encountered them before. In synthesizing their ideas into short pieces, we hope to provide you with an accessible alternative (or starting point) to work by these authority figures, and a bitesize format means you can dip in and out rather than having to read it chronologically.

Our guests may have mostly been at home in our first year of recording, but that was all they had in common. Their variety of professional backgrounds, from philosophy and public policy to law and engineering, their sixty-two-year age range (Sneha Revanur was sixteen at the time; N. Katherine Hayles was seventy-seven) and a variety of geographical locations (from and between the UK, India, Nigeria, Germany, the USA, Canada, Puerto Rico, and Thailand) result in complementary and conflictual viewpoints on what "good technology" might entail. The majority of contributors are currently based in the United States, which reflects the state of funding on AI issues and gives insight into where discussions around feminism and technology are most prominent (as well as which geographical locations tend to get prioritized in the global conversation about AI). The contributors often discuss their diasporic positions and the diasporic nature of technology itself—or, how people and technologies move across borders and operate through them. They also draw feminist thinkers across space, time, and disciplines to interrogate their ideas: from Asian and Asian diaspora feminisms and Black feminist thought to queer theory and indigenous thinkers. Where the sheer volume and range of pro-justice approaches to technology can be overwhelming, this collection brings together a variety of perspectives from postcolonial studies, disability theory, and critical race studies to confront ageism, racism, sexism, ableism, and class-based oppressions in AI. The volume showcases the variety of feminist approaches to technology that we curate in the podcast, which span generations, continents, and disciplines.

This reflects our own expansive definition of feminism. While as the last of our three good tech questions we ask interviewees "how can feminism help us get there?" we occasionally approach feminism from the perspective of disability theory, critical race theory, or another social justice-oriented approach. To us, these are very much part of feminism's scope; if feminism is about achieving justice and equality for women (including, without any shadow of a doubt, trans* women) and gender minorities, how can it hope to meaningfully engage with all aspects of women's gendered experiences without grappling with how gender is entwined with so many other aspects of power and social justice? Our feminist approach is fundamentally *intersectional*, a Black feminist concept put forward by the Combahee River Collective, Kimberlé Crenshaw and Patricia Hill Collins (among others) that shows how oppressions such as sexism, racism, homophobia, transphobia, classism, ableism, and ageism are intertwined and cannot be easily separated out from each other. We also see feminism as a collective project: as the Black feminist bell hooks famously wrote, feminism is for everybody.

That being said, while we think that feminism can certainly help us get closer to good technology, we do not think that everybody's feminism looks the same, or that feminism lays down the same road for everyone to get there. What matters, though, is that feminism itself—like our concept of the good robot—continues to be *provocative*: that it continues to compel us to question the unequal and unjust status quo, and advocate for and imagine radically better worlds. It sometimes feels a bit taboo to ask people about feminism in tech spaces, and that would probably be reason enough to keep insisting on the question. When writing their book *Data Feminism*, Catherine D'Ignazio and Lauren Klein were often asked why they had to use the term feminism. Why not something like data *justice* instead? In a moment where there is still an awkwardness around the term, gender-based violence remains pervasive and systemic, and encroachment on fundamental gender-based human rights like abortion is on the rise, this book is proof that feminism must still be an integral part of social justice thinking. While perspectives on what feminism can do in technology vary—and not always because of generational and geographic differences—we use this book as an opportunity to draw alliances as our response to the divisions of today.

Each of our contributors was asked to respond to the brief "good technology is X." We have grouped the resulting chapters into four headings: Good Relations, Good Systems, Good Designs, Good Visions, and Good Rebellions. In Good Relations, the chapters explore how we can live well with and alongside technology, and what good relations with AI and other new and emerging technologies look like. In "Good Relations," Blaise Agüera y Arcas, Jason Edward Lewis, N. Katherine Hayles, Rosi Braidotti, and Sneha Revanur explore how good technology includes and reflects our relationships with each other and with the world around us. In "Good Systems" Wendy Hui Kyong Chun, Margaret Mitchell, Soraj Hongladarom, Jennifer Lee, and hannah holtzclaw suggest how both technical systems and wider social and political systems must simultaneously be reoriented towards justice. In "Good Designs," Os Keyes, David Adelani, Ranjit Singh, Priya Goswami and Meryl Alper examine how feminist ethics should be embedded in the design process. In "Good Visions," Neda Atanasoski and Felicity Amaya Schaeffer, Anne Anlin Cheng, Michele Elam, and Kanta Dihal show us the problems with how we currently talk about and imagine technology, and provide us with more hopeful narratives. Finally, in "Good Rebellions," Catherine D'Ignazio, Frances Negrón-Mutaner, Kate Chandler, and Jack Halberstam explain how sometimes moving toward good technology means stepping away from others, and that while good technology might not always be possible, good rebellions certainly are.

Most of all, we hope that this quickfire journey through the world of gender, feminism, and technology serves as a provocation for *you*. We want these chapters to challenge you, inspire you, show you different ways of thinking about technology and the world around you. We do not want you to be naive about the real and often horrifying risks posed by new technologies, but we do not want you to feel hopefully frightened by them either. Instead, we want you to walk away from this volume feeling that while good technology may be difficult—some might say, even impossible—perhaps feminism can help us work some of the way toward it.

Part I

Good Relations

Eleanor Drage

What does it mean to seek new ways of relating at a time when we are algorithmically encouraged to harden ourselves to each other? For philosophers like Paul Gilroy, we need to establish communities that go beyond identity politics and tribalism, and are instead based in "will, inclination, mood, and affinity." These are delicate, generous, and expansive kinds of connections. But how does this work in practice? Can we really change where and how we think we belong? In *Poetics of Relation*, the celebrated Martinican poet Edouard Glissant argues in powerful, lyrical prose that Relating (with a capital 'R') to one another involves a rerouting of the forms of connection that we think we desire. The chapters in this part give us concrete examples of how this rerouting works. It is not easy, and it involves wandering off the beaten track to establish solidarities that can often be uncomfortable and difficult to maintain.

While often we believe that we relate better to those who are from the same place as us or have a similar background, Glissant tells us that Relation isn't about anchoring ourselves to a singular, geographically dependent root but exploring our shifting positions in dense networks of information. These networks have been called "rhizomes" by French philosophers Gilles Deleuze and Felix Guattari. Scholars have likened rhizomes to the delicate spread of nerves in an eyeball, and the roots of an orchid that float on water without anchoring themselves to the ground. Identity, like these networks, is not a fixed thing, but is shaped by our relationships with people. Abuse them, and the nerve filaments burst, obstructing connections and the healthy flow of information.

In this part, our contributors explore different ways of identifying with each other and relating to the nonhuman world. In an era when we're encouraged to sum ourselves up in a 160-character Twitter bio or vicious 300-character rebuttal, technology quickens the speed at which we point fingers at each other and say, "I know exactly what sort of person you are." These technologies can harden ourselves to people of different opinions, binding us instead to uncomplex views and interests. We were already brutal to each other before social media, and now we can exacerbate these behaviors at speed and scale. It is tempting to see all this and feel an urge to shut ourselves off from the world. And yet, we are asked by the contributors to try harder to relate to each other, to uproot what we might think of as our single sources of identity and search for belonging in unfamiliar and surprising places.

This involves making some detours in our usual ways of establishing who we are. If we keep our identities moving, it will allow us to be moved by each other and by the world. All these chapters create this kind of movement and ask us to be emotionally stirred. Of course, being open and empathetic to each other requires some humility. We often think we know others, that we can label and make statements about a generation or a demographic. We need to walk away from this way of thinking by not assuming that we can know everything about each other. This unknowable side of the world is in Glissant's words its "threatened beauty."

1

Good Technology Is Cooperative

Blaise Agüera y Arcas

Blaise leads Cerebra, a Google Research organization working on computer vision, machine intelligence, and computational photography. We first clocked Blaise's feminist perspectives when we listened to him combat some unsavory views on intelligence and evolution on another podcast. He handled the debate with poise and gentleness, using clear examples aided by an extraordinary breadth of knowledge. Rather you than me, Eleanor thought, listening, glad that Blaise was on-side to negotiate with social Darwinist perspectives on AI. In 2017, his investment in debunking harmful myths around AI came good again, when, with coauthors Margaret Mitchell and Alexander Todorov, he published a piece debunking sexuality recognition software. The trio used their knowledge of machine learning to show that the system wasn't "recognizing" sexuality but other elements of the photos that it correlated with. There are many ways to debunk these kinds of products, but Kerry and I are grateful for the people who carry enough technical knowledge and industry respect to change minds and hearts.

We urgently need to move toward an understanding of good technology as *cooperative rather than competitive.*

To understand why the competitive mindset is so deeply ingrained, consider the way utilitarianism and its mathematical expression—*optimization*—has been central to so much modern technology, including AI. At first glance, this doesn't seem like a problem. A bicycle wheel might be optimized for lightness and rigidity under torque; an image classifier might be optimized to correctly classify images.

As a mathematical tool, optimization can be useful, but as a grand principle, it can mislead, or even harm. We think of "optimal" as meaning "good," or even "the best." But is life a competition at being "the best"? Best at what, and in what context? That nature is an engine for optimization, that we humans are the smartest, and therefore the most "optimal," and that such optimality equals "goodness" are ideas worth debunking. They are not just wrong because they imply abhorrent ethics (for instance, eugenics) but because they are not scientifically—or even mathematically—sound.

Let's begin with the myth that humans are primarily motivated by outperforming each other and other creatures by being the smartest. This myth fuels the belief that our relationship with machines will be fundamentally competitive, for are we not trying to make AI that is even smarter than we are? Hence the fear that superintelligent AI will wipe out humans in its quest for supremacy. Maybe this explains why we continue to be obsessed with Terminator-like fantasies of artificial general intelligence (AGI) enslaving humanity. This strikes me as a paranoid and improbable scenario.

To be clear, I am not a techno-optimist—I don't believe that technology is automatically good, nor that it is automatically bad. Design matters; more to the point, design always proceeds from a designer's perspective. All entities with anything like agency—not just individual people but other animals, sports teams, companies, countries, political parties, ant colonies, entire species—relate to each other in a social graph.

When it comes to humans (and their digital kin), technology mediates many of those interactions. This can have all sorts of effects, positive, and negative, depending on your perspective. As a technology maker, I try to step back and ask what sorts of tweaks or modifications to the technology might help or harm the parties in these interactions. One can strive for impartiality, but it is not possible to take a truly utilitarian standpoint by creating an equation for the most harm or the most good. How would that even be calculated? Not all entities are equivalent, and there is no view from nowhere; moreover the technology maker is also an actor in this network. None of us should pretend to be a disinterested party.

Margaret Thatcher famously claimed that there is no such thing as society, only individuals. However, it is impossible to reduce groups to the sum of the individuals in them. (Even Thatcher amended in her next breath, "and there are families.") Whenever we analyze discrimination, for instance, we necessarily encounter a *collective* harm. If we were to redistribute the harms done to members of a certain community uniformly across the wider population, then according to a utilitarian or individualistic perspective, it would be awash; the total harm would remain unchanged. But obviously these situations are not equivalent. Discrimination or injustice, oppression or privilege, implies benefit and harm to collective entities. Any notion of justice requires differentiating between random and discriminatory distributions of harms, even if they sum up to the same total when tallied over individuals.

Collectivity in humans has powerful and ancient biological origins. For instance, anthropologist and primatologist Sarah Hrdy has written extensively about alloparenting: meaning baby care provided by individuals other than parents.[1] She describes alloparenting as a key human trait differentiating us from the other apes. We need "babysitters" to help rear our young; a mother on her own cannot produce the thirteen million calories that it takes to raise a child to self-sufficiency. Humans have adaptive and cooperative childrearing strategies, which Hrdy argues have played a central role in the way we have become good at seeing things from each other's point of view and emotionally invest in each other. We can call this *intersubjectivity*. Such empathy and mutual aid were probably essential to our survival during the last Ice Age, and enabled our dramatic development after the glaciers retreated. It has taken a lot of teamwork.

Cooperative
We have become good at seeing things from each other's point of view and emotionally invest in each other.

Intelligence and creativity rely on intersubjectivity too. As with ethics, though, if we only think in terms of one-to-one relationships, we miss much of the picture. Our obsession with intelligence as an individual property residing in a single brain is a particularly Western take. It's related to the way we tend to attribute art to an individual artist, a singular inspired mind whose works, too, are singular. That is an illusion. Lothar Ledderose, a German professor of the History of Art of Eastern Asia, documents counterexamples in his book *Ten Thousand Things: Module and Mass Production in Chinese Art*.[2] Ledderose studies artifacts like the terracotta warrior army of Qin Shi Huang, the first emperor of China, and the monumental temples of Cambodia. These works of art cannot be attributed in any meaningful way to a single artist. Does that mean they are not art? Surely they are. When image-generating neural nets like Dall-E and Midjourney win art prizes, it is hard not to conclude that the same goes for modern Western artistic traditions too! Like creativity, intelligence operates across entire networks, and is often not the product of any single human brain. Even when it appears to be, that brain is shaped by the cumulative output of an entire culture, just like the neural nets powering Dall-E and Midjourney.

Competitiveness
Our obsession with intelligence as an individual property residing in a single brain.

But we must widen our view even further. The intelligence that humans tap into is the product of a multi-species ecosystem that *includes* technology. While some transhumanist thinkers (like Nick Bostrom) claim that one day humans will become superintelligent when they merge with technology,[3] I think we have always crossed that threshold. As Australian performance artist Stelarc says, "technology is what defines the meaning of being human, it's part of being human."[4] There are literal examples, like the fact that we have short guts because we invented fire and so could cook food; fire has therefore come back around and shaped our bodies. The same is true of our lack of body hair: our clothes *are* our body hair. That's why (although I am not a fan of much of today's big agribusiness) I think it is a fallacy for people to insist on "natural" foods over GMOs. Most of the food we eat is heavily engineered, and it has been for around

10,000 years. In fact we have been "engineering" our foods and ourselves for a lot longer than 10,000 years—probably closer to seven million.

Another way of thinking about technology is as an inorganic extrusion of our intelligence, growing out of us much the same way a snail's shell grows out of a snail. Technology remains bound up with humanity, just as the shell is bound up with its snail. AI makes it clear how technology augments not only our bodies but also our minds. Then again, you can think about language as a technology that has been augmenting our minds for hundreds of thousands of years (as well as our bodies, for in another example of co-evolution with technology, we have developed a far richer vocal gamut than our primate brethren).

Because I do not see a boundary between humans and technology, I have always been puzzled by the idea of "othering" technology that we tend to see in dystopian narratives about computers taking over. In the twentieth century, some people imagined that machines were so powerful, so influential that they heard voices coming from the television set telling them what to do. This form of schizophrenia (the "Influencing Machine") has existed throughout history. It represents a misattribution of agency. It isn't that we *are not* influenced by the TV, but it would be equally absurd to suppose that our free will has ever been wholly individual. Ideas like will and agency are hard to even formulate outside a social context. So, free will has been mixed up with technology for as long as technology has mediated social interactions.

We are guilty of a similar misunderstanding when we talk about AI "wanting" to be independent from or in competition with humanity. We are always competing and collaborating with each other in all kinds of ways. So the idea of technology as being "other," as alien, seems like an autoimmune disorder of the mind. Why do we have paranoid fantasies about AI as a bogeyman rather than as a distributed intelligence that is always mixed in with humanity? Indeed, modern AI is created by training large models on large corpuses of human interaction. What further evidence do we need that intelligence is social, that it literally resides *in* those interactions?

Paranoid fantasies about AI are related to our "othering" of what we call "the environment"—as if we could exist separate from it. We need a cooperative view of evolution and intelligence that takes stock of the complexity of humanity's relationship to its ecosystem, both natural and technological—if, indeed, such a distinction is even meaningful. Overlooking cooperation and focusing only on competition has misled many into thinking that humans are "programmed" to dominate nature and each other in order to survive. Domination is not in fact nature's "loss function" (what it is optimized for), and neither is it the "loss function" of any AI I know of. It is not a known route to intelligence.

Survival is often interpreted in a winner-takes-all utilitarian framework where humans or AIs are trying to progress at any cost. I have heard people bring up Charles Darwin and Herbert Spencer's ideas about life being optimized for survival to make it seem like the death of other species is favorable to humans because it creates more space in the ecosystem for them. Ecological, empirical, mathematical, and economic arguments all negate such a view. Put simply, life depends on other life, and rich, resilient ecosystems are necessarily diverse. Even Darwin realized it. In fact, the utilitarian, zero-sum, optimization-obsessed approach came more from Spencer than from Darwin.[5] When people talk about survival of the fittest, we might ask, survival of what? Are the cells in our bodies optimized this way, for instance? They have to work together to keep us alive; they're not optimized for individual survival. The cells in our gut have a very short life span, but they are surely a part of us. Our bodies are dynamic systems with many timescales. Insofar as evolution is a selection process, it selects for systems that are *dynamically stable* over many scales.

Conversely, there is often nothing particularly "optimal" about the crazy things that nature has produced: the tail of a peacock, the mane of a lion, all these weird and beautiful excesses. The problem is in fact the notion of optimality itself. Thinking about life in terms of optimizing some function only works if you imagine that we exist in a fixed single-player game with an unchanging environment. This is how DeepMind began: with single-player Atari games. Then, "good" and "bad" play are easy to define; they are quantified by a score. Likewise with chess or AlphaGo, where there are two opposing players whose rules are the same, with one winning and the other losing. But real life is not a chess match with predefined rules, or a video game in a fixed environment. Neither are we trying to "beat" nature by, for example, reproducing as much as possible in order to attain the largest possible population—the myth that has informed fears of AI "taking over," and doing the same to us. Let's agree that human extinction would be bad. But humans will not be happy campers if there are a hundred billion of us living on a depleted planet, sustained by technical life support systems, with every other species extinct. How could such an outcome possibly be "good," from *any* point of view?

Notes

1 Sarah Blaffer Hrdy, Mothers and Others, *The Evolutionary Origins of Mutual Understanding* (Cambridge: Harvard University Press, 2011).

2 Lothar Ledderose, *Ten Thousand Things: Module and Mass Production in Chinese Art* (Princeton: Princeton University Press, 2001).

3 Nick Bostrom, *Superintelligence: Paths, Dangers, Strategies* (Oxford: Oxford University Press, 2014).

4 Paolo Atzori and Kirk Woolford, "Extended-Body: Interview with Stelarc," in *Digital Delirium*, ed. Arthur Kroker and Marilouise Kroker (London: Palgrave Macmillan, 1997), 94–199.

5 Peter Kropotkin, *Mutual Aid: A Factor in Evolution* (London: William Heinemann, 1902), 14.

2

Good Technology Is Messy

Jason Edward Lewis

Jason's generosity, sense of fun, and larger-than-life personality makes him not only a great podcast guest but an extraordinary community-builder and teacher. He's careful to reference the contributions of younger academics to his work and point to the perspectives of others who have influenced his thinking. As University Research Chair in Computational Media and the Indigenous Future Imaginary and Professor of Computation Arts at Concordia University, Jason brings together computation with art, futurism, and Indigenous knowledges. He's spent fifteen years exploring how Indigenous people use digital technologies to tell stories, and more broadly, how communication technologies affect how we understand one another and the world around us.

Good technology is messy, because good technology is responsive to local human context. And, goodness, humans are messy. Without a doubt, we have benefited mightily from technologies designed to be deployed at scale, to be used by tens of thousands, millions, and hundreds of millions of people across the world. But as we have scaled technology we have overwritten many things that are important to local communities. We can define "local communities" in many different ways, but in my work that means Indigenous communities. There are many different Indigenous communities—Kānaka Maoli, Kanien'kehá:ka, Lakȟóta—with members living on their territory, in cities nearby or distant, or internationally, like me as a Kānaka Maoli person living in Montreal.

Developing good technology means getting away from the assumption that all users are in some way alike, and that the user can be universalized into a limited number of user profiles. Design generally, and Human-Computer

Interaction (HCI) design in particular, tends to group potential users into a few categories and use those personas to design something that will, theoretically, appeal to most people. This process rarely takes into account the cultural dimension of people's lives. But culture is central: we cannot understand individuals without understanding their culture, or the cultures that they emerge from, and those that they aspire to inhabit. I am not talking about an inherently conservative way of looking at cultural provenance, where you assume that just because I grew up as an adopted-out Kānaka Maoli in Northern California this is going to determine everything about me for the rest of my life. It is part of me, but it is also everything that has happened to me since then, all the different communities that I have stepped into that have made me who I am, and also the different ways of being that I experiment with as I grow older. So while all these wonderful computational tools derive much of their power from being deployed at scale, we need to minimize the harm that is done by them as they abstract individuals into categories. We do this by paying much closer attention to the specific circumstances in which they are used, where culture and the community play a central role.

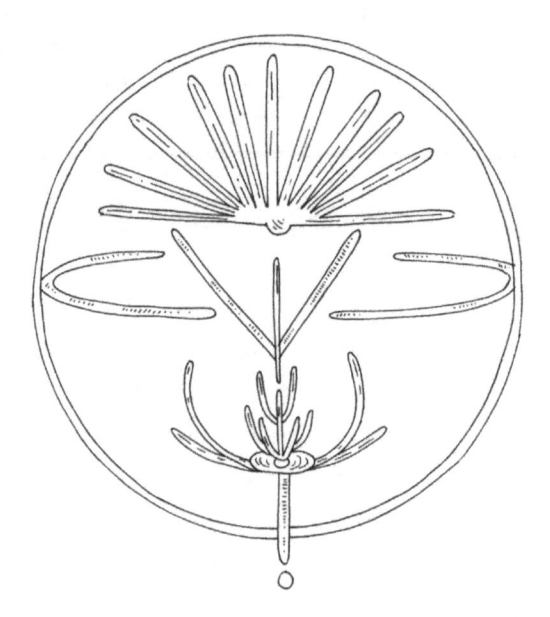

Unity
Developing good technology means getting away from the assumption that all users are in some way alike, and that the user can be universalized into a limited number of user profiles.

Paying attention to how culture shapes our relationship with technology can also help us rethink how humans and machines should coexist. Indigenous cultures are able to talk about nonhumans in a respectful and generative way. This is partly because they are not operating out of the English language, which is a tool shaped heavily by its evolution within a Western tradition saturated with Christian values and positivist knowledge practices. It is almost impossible, from an English-language perspective, to talk about nonhumans as being on par with humans. The Anglophone tradition places man at the center of our world, and everything else is subordinate, less than. The Scientific Revolution and the Enlightenment both made very strong, monotheistic claims that the framework they generated provided the only true route to knowing the world. If you operate through other belief systems you are considered irrational or, worse, an intellectual heretic: unclean and impure. This creates many conceptual obstacles when looking to nonhumans for knowledge, because it is assumed that only humans generate and hold knowledge. Anytime we start talking about having conversations with trees or fish it automatically gets pushed into either a spiritual or "junk science" register. It differs too much from how "rational scientists" talk. This makes it difficult, in the Western intellectual context, to see the full extent of what relationships might be between humans and nonhumans, or even between nonhumans. We have to look to other traditions to widen our conceptual boundaries.

Ideas are embedded in our languages, ways of being and knowing, and in our cosmologies that ease the path toward closer relationships with nonhumans. Of course, there is an incredibly diverse approach to human/nonhuman relationships across Indigenous cultures. The PhD candidate with whom I work, Suzanne Kite, notes that her people, the Lakota, believe that all stones are capable of speaking—but only some will speak to you. Other Indigenous traditions think differently, that stones are not our relations but are nevertheless an important part of our world. Indigenous traditions vary. Indigenous languages have specific ways of articulating the relationships between creatures, retaining a flexibility for and complex nuance when addressing them; an understanding of who can talk with them; descriptions of the appropriate and effective protocols for those conversations; and the stories that document previous conversations that help us relate to them today.

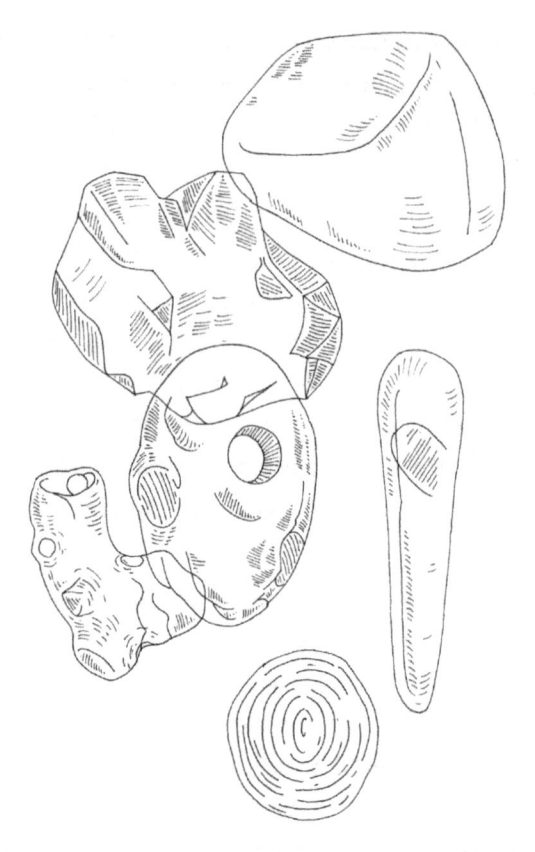

Multiplicity
All stones are capable of speaking—but only some will speak to you.

Engaging with an abundance of knowledge systems also allows us to think differently about what we mean by intelligence. In mainstream AI research and development, intelligence has arguably collapsed into very narrow approaches. Machine learning (ML), the current dominant mode of doing AI, has eaten the AI world and made itself synonymous with AI. When ML practitioners are writing as scientists, they make it very clear that ML is just one approach. However, when they are talking to the press, or trying to get money, that distinction goes out the window. You get coverage and cash if you say "AI" but not so much if you say "statistics," which is basically what ML is. The industry has converged on a definition of intelligence which is probably best summarized as rational goal-seeking. It is an incredibly narrow definition that does not take into account the many different ways in which we behave intelligently in the world.

There is a long history to this argument. Howard Gardner made this point in the 1980s in *Frames of Mind: The Theory of Multiple Intelligences*. Some of the debates around that time were really about different kinds of intelligences and how they operate differently and how we need to understand these differences. How can we formalize these modes of intelligence and make them computable so that we can embed them in machines? But most of those ideas got pushed aside when ML really took off about a decade ago, when they finally had the right equipment to make it feasible to work at scale.

But it is dangerous to have only one approach to intelligence. I am trying to understand what it means to consider intelligence from the perspectives of my own Indigenous community (and—full disclosure—I am really just at the beginning stages of learning what "my own community" means). It is useful to take seriously the idea that what makes someone an intelligent member of the Hawaiian community is not necessarily the same thing as what it means to be considered an intelligent member of American society. One culture's wise person is another culture's fool.

We need to ask what it means to act in the world in a way that contributes not only to your own well-being but to the well-being of the community around you and to the territory on which you find yourself. None of the standard AI models are capable of dealing with that kind of complexity. I am not convinced they will ever be able to incorporate it. I am not sure if the way we are going about modeling behavior actually allows us to reflect on the complexity of being in the world. That is frightening. We are building these incredible, crazy technologies to emulate ourselves without first understanding ourselves. The reason we are going to end up with Skynet is not because Skynet will wake up one day and randomly decide that it is going to kill humans. It is because we are building sociopathic robots, machines that do not understand what is important to real humans.

This is why we need a different perspective on how to make tech less harmful. When we focus on technical fixes to "bias" in our computational systems, we are missing the big picture. We correct bias on a case-by-case basis without looking at the underlying problems that relate to economic selfishness, social inequalities, historical racism, all these different dynamics that structure the world. But there is a big difference between mathematical models of bias and the real world. A system can be working properly from a computational standpoint and still be horribly biased in its consequences. Often, people building these systems make an appeal to the law—it is legal!—or to customer desire—everybody wants one! They use these rationales to escape responsibility. Because there is so much money to be made in AI innovation, we allow AI engineers to disregard social harms in ways that we would never let a civil engineer get away with.

Computational systems are a reflection of our value systems. This is why you must have a diverse set of people in the room when you design technologies that will impact large numbers of people. If you work with a homogenous project team you get locked into your own assumptions and you make devices that people outside of your bubble would look at and say, "Wow, that is really stupid." Or harmful. But inside your team, you have convinced each other that it is the greatest thing ever, who would not want this device sitting on their kitchen table? Engineers and funders seem to think, for example, that self-driving cars are the most exciting thing that we can do with the incredible brain power and amounts of money at our disposal. I am thinking about the slogan that emerged when all the billionaires went into space this year: we need better billionaires. God, the current crop lacks imagination! They are just fulfilling a Western science fiction fantasy that is 100 years old. I still know people in Silicon Valley, funders and engineers, and I often wonder, are you guys not bored out of your skull? At a micro-level, we can all lose ourselves in technical challenges that are deeply fascinating. But at the macro-level—at which I would hope that kind of money would allow you to operate—I just really wonder sometimes what they are so excited about.

I am not making an argument against technology: most of the Indigenous people with whom I work want to take advantage of these technologies. As Indigenous people we have survived by adapting to new technologies as well as developing our own. So our question is, how do we adapt this technology to better suit us now? In the long term, how can we grow our communities' capacity to build systems from the ground up that reflect the ways in which we want to live? We want intelligent entities that help us, work with us, play with us, create with us, and show us ways of understanding and looking at the world that we currently have little or no access to.

ML and Big Data Science are really good at seeing patterns that are either too small or too large for us humans to really apprehend. Even if we can see them, we cannot readily manipulate them on our own to figure out what they mean. But perhaps working with these tools has much in common with having a vision. Visions can be described as seeing patterns in the flow of life around you that you cannot see in everyday life. What is exciting about AI is that it can see things that I cannot see. These machines are part of our reality—they are helping co-construct reality with us—and we should be excited about having another perspective, because reality is a complicated place, and the more we learn, the more complex it becomes. Life was supposed to get simpler—mathematics and physics were supposed to have converged into a unified model of the world that would explain everything. We understand now that there cannot be a complete mathematical system that can prove everything we know to be true; we suspect that there are aspects of quantum mechanics that will always be beyond our ability to understand. To me, this is glorious! It is not like this has kept us from making useful stuff. It is beautiful that the world is messy. It is that messiness that suggests, strongly, that the more perspectives we bring to our attempts to understand our world, the better off we will be, the more of the world we will be able to grasp, the better relation we will be to the hon-human beings around us, and the more of human experience we will be able to honor when we build technology.

3

Good Technology Is Biophilic

N. Katherine Hayles

The star of science and technology studies and author of How We Became Posthuman *and* My Mother Was a Computer, *it seemed very unlikely that the eminent N. Katherine Hayles would accept to be on The Good Robot. As you'll see from the references to her throughout this collection, she's a guiding light to many people working in technology, feminism, and philosophy. Hayles has by her own admission been a feminist for over half a century, and it is very much an integrated part of her worldview. As such, it has informed her groundbreaking work, forging what was at the time the entirely new field of literature and science. Convinced that* Unthought, *her latest book on consciousness, would be the perfect antidote to dominant ways of thinking about human and machine brains in AI spaces, we were desperate to have her on the podcast. Hayles was one of our first guests, looked very smart, was extremely gracious when we had a major technical mishap, lost Kerry in the podcast vortex, and then panic-emailed her when we thought we had lost her recording. A true star in all senses of the word.*

A good human-technology relationship is one that foregrounds human relationality and recognizes that humans are interconnected with each other, with nonhuman species, and with the planet. Feminism involves an orientation to the environment and to the planet that is "biophilic"—which implies reaching beyond humans to the nonhuman world. My recent book *Unthought* focused on the idea of cognitive assemblages, distributed cognition and distributed agency. Part of the argument that I was making was about the cognitive capacities of nonhuman living beings. I argue that all life-forms possess cognitive capacities; moreover, many artificial entities, for example neural nets, possess cognitive capacities as well.

Biophilic
Reaching beyond humans to the non-human world.

I was looking for a definition of cognition that would have a low threshold for something to count as cognitive, yet scale up to include something as complex as human consciousness. Here is what I came up with: "Cognition is a process of interpreting information in contexts that connect it with meaning."[1] Meaning is to be understood here as reaching beyond verbal or symbolic representations, to include behaviors that nonconscious organisms perform in response to environmental stimuli. Not only does this open cognition up to the more-than-human world; it also implies that all cognitive entities, even plants and bacteria, are capable of meaning-making practices because they sense their environments and respond accordingly. As Lynn Margulis, the microbiologist who revolutionized evolutionary biology, observed: "All living beings, not just animals but plants and microorganisms, perceive. To survive, an organic being must perceive—it must seek, or at least recognize, food and avoid environmental danger."[2] No doubt the organism's responses to such stimuli are meaningful to it, inasmuch as they help the organism to continue its existence.

One of the great challenges of our era is to find ways to integrate these nonhuman cognizers into our psychological, social, and economic schemes without losing the human values that I think should be paramount in those relationships. Artificial cognizers (thinkers), such as contemporary neural nets, pose special challenges. Artificial "cognizers" (thinkers) are vastly different from humans in many respects; I will mention just two here. One is the time scale at which they operate. Artificial entities move at enormously faster speeds than humans can. The second issue that I emphasize is the difference between how humans and AIs are embodied (given bodies—made visible and tangible). Sometimes people speak of AIs as though these cognizers don't have bodies, but of course they all have bodies; it is impossible to exist without having a body. It's just that they're embodied in radically different ways than humans, which leads to many misunderstandings, misrepresentations, and misalliances.

How do we move forward in this complex environment? I think this is particularly difficult for North Americans because we have a tradition of individualism and self-reliance. One of the first things we have to accept is that in the contemporary world, cognition and agency are distributed. We can begin to come to terms with our contemporary condition as participants in cognitive assemblages by setting aside traditionally prized qualities like free will, individualism, and self-reliance. It is not that they are altogether irrelevant but they don't serve us very well in environments where cognition and agency are distributed. The sooner we accept the fact that we are not the only cognizers on the planet, the better off we will be.

Feminism is absolutely crucial here because there have been many feminist studies that have shown that the tendency to abstract from embodied realities has typically been a masculinist pursuit, and that women in general have been denigrated because we are associated with the body and with more earthly things like giving birth and so on, whereas masculine intellect is celebrated precisely because it is removed from those womanly essential values. So yes, feminism is crucial. But I think the problem actually goes deeper than that. It stems from the very human tendency of wanting to project an anthropocentric personality or subjectivity onto anything that is recognized as having cognitive abilities. We see this with animals, certainly. But we see it also with technological objects, which are increasingly responsive, autonomous, and intelligent on their own.

One area of my current research has to do with deep fakes. As you may know, deep fakes use generative antagonistic networks (GANs) to learn, over and over again, the voice patterns, movements, and other elusive qualities that enable humans to communicate. They then use these to create a video, still image, or some other technological artifact that has the face of, for example, a celebrity pasted onto a porn star body performing sexual acts. Deep fakes can be used in a multitude of ways. Not all of these are bad; some are amusing and some are used for entertainment. But it does raise deep questions about how we evaluate whether another being is conscious. Right now, as far as I know, there are no artificial entities that are conscious. They are responsive; they can perform cognitive acts, for sure. And they can model consciousness given the proper algorithms. But, of course, that is different from actually being conscious.

This is a famous problem in philosophy. How do I know that someone is conscious? How do I know that you are conscious? How do I know that I am conscious? The practical answer has always been that I am aware of myself thinking and so, because of this self-awareness, I know that I'm conscious. Because you're a human like me, I can make the assumption that you're conscious as well. But what happens when we encounter an artificial entity consisting of a simulacrum, a representation or imitation that is amazingly like another human being but is completely lacking in consciousness? It is possible that some art forms, for example novels, cannot exist without portraying consciousness. Even the "it" novels popular in the eighteenth century featured narrators (pins, buttons, currency, medals) who spoke as if they were conscious. What would a novel devoid of representations of conscious beings look like? Dennis Tenen has written about novels that have nonconscious entities as their protagonists (*Airport, Hotel,* etc.), but there are still lots of conscious humans to carry the action.[3]

The challenge for a writer is how you can depict an artificial entity which is not conscious but has high cognitive abilities. To date, I know of no successful novel that has done that. I can give you lots of novels that presume the artificial entity is conscious, and then go on to speculate what artificial consciousness would be like. In my article "Subversion of the Human Aura: A Crisis in Representation" (2023), I analyze three such novels from the perspective of how they anticipate that human-AI relations will evolve: Annalee Newitz's *Autonomous*, Kuzuo Ishiguro's *Klara and the Sun*, and Ian McEwan's *Machines like Me*. These are valuable explorations of some of the ethical, political, and psychological issues that will emerge when (or rather, if) conscious AI entities become possible. But they don't shed light on a contemporary problem confronting us right now: How do we deal with entities that are profoundly different from us in embodiment but that are capable of generating human-level languages and discourses?

I am thinking here of large language models such as Google's LaMDA (Language Model for Dialogue Applications) and GPT-3 (Generative Pretrained Transformer, version 3). These are huge neural net programs that have been trained on petabytes of human-written texts (it is estimated that a petabyte is equivalent to *500 billion* pages of printed standard texts). GPT-3 has billions of parameters and has made millions (at least) of inferences about how human languages work and consequently about human cultures. GPT-3 can not only analyze and reproduce anyone's literary style, from Mark Twain to the King James Bible, but can also grasp high-level qualities such as literary genres. There is no unmistakable indication so far that the program is conscious, but it clearly has formidable analytical abilities and can respond to queries and commands with several pages of coherent, semantically correct texts. LaMDA, optimized to engage in dialogues with humans, has already convinced a Google engineer, Blake Lemoine, that it *is* conscious—an opinion that, when he went public with it, got him fired by Google.

On the other side are skeptics such as Emily Bender and colleagues, who have called such programs "stochastic parrots,"[4] producing texts devoid of meaning except for what humans project onto them. The truth is that we simply do not have good strategies to deal with texts like those generated by GPT-3 and LaMDA. In my experience, a close reading of these machine-generated texts reveals that they are far more than simple repetitions of the texts on which they were trained, for they show considerable inventiveness and often devise clever rhetorical strategies. On the other hand, I think it is a mistake to treat them as if they are the same as human-generated texts. They emerge from radically different embodiments and umwelten (or world-horizons) distinctive to the architectures and textual experiences of these machines. In contrast to any human who has ever lived, these machines have no direct sensory experience of the real world; all they know are languages and representations (this may change, however, as plans are already in progress to couple these programs with sensors and actuators so they can experience the world through their distinctive worldly capacities). In my view, we should regard these machine-generated texts as the products of highly advanced cognizers with embodiments distinctively different from humans. If they are not conscious, nevertheless the enormous number of inferences they make may constitute an intermediate stage that we could call proto-sentient. They may be equivalent to *Homo habilus* in human evolution—harbingers or evolutionary predecessors of a true artificial general intelligence (AGI) with capabilities equivalent or superior to those of humans.

The scary part of this is that our understanding of how we should relate to such intelligent machines lags far behind our abilities to create them. What ethical guidelines should constrain such machines? How could these guidelines be enforced, given the premise that an AGI is as smart or smarter than humans? What are our ethical responsibilities to such machines? These are questions that may inevitably confront us before there is anything like a consensus about what the answers should be.

In order to achieve a general understanding of the issues involved, we need to foster good relationships between humanities scholars, artists, critical thinkers, and the people who make technology. I have had numerous encounters with engineers, roboticists, and so forth and I've always found them very welcoming. I will add a caveat here. If you are a humanist, like me, you can't expect them to show up at your office; you have to go to where they live and hang out. You have to make the first move, and ask, "Can I come visit you in your lab?" Once you're there, you can begin to pose questions, and on the basis of that, you may be able to make suggestions, possibly intervening at the point where designs are still being forged and thought through. That is where true ethical thinking has to take place, rather than trying to add it on at the end, as if it were icing on the cake. No, it has to be baked in from the beginning[5].

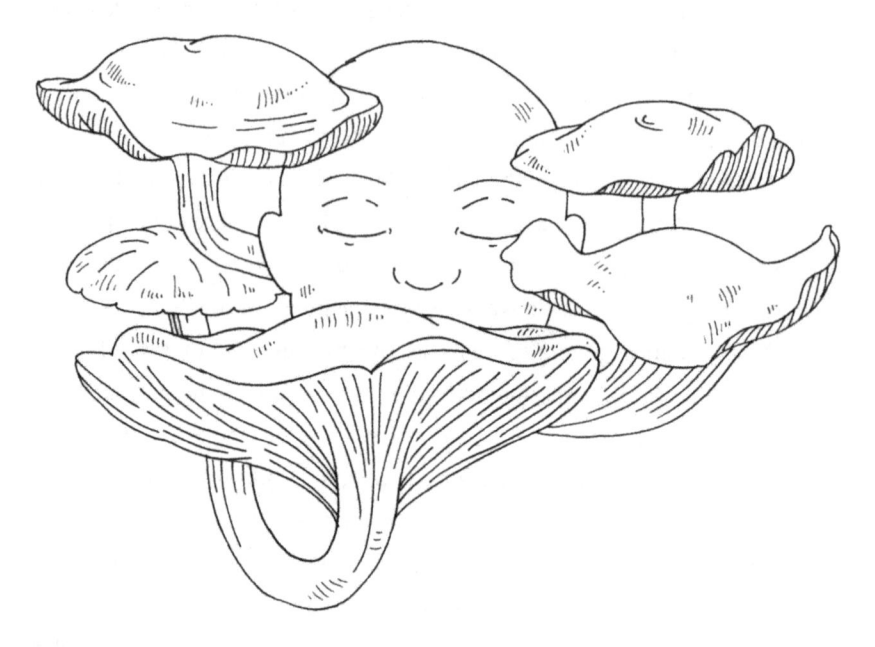

Humanist
You have to make the first move, and ask, "Can I come visit you in your lab?" Once you're there, you can begin to pose questions . . . possibly intervening at the point where designs are still being forged and thought through.

If those prerequisites are met, along with attitudes of mutual respect, my experience has been that technical people are more than happy to talk to you about their work. They are thrilled that you are interested and they will be quite open to suggestions. Of course, not all your suggestions are going to be useful because you may lack the technical knowledge. But they are the beginning, the basis, the foundation for further enlightening exchanges. To my mind, this is one promising route to ensuring that our technologies are good for humans and nonhumans alike.

Notes

1   N. Katherine Hayles, *Postprint: Books and Becoming Computational* (New York: Columbia University Press, 2021), 6.

2   Lynn Margulis and Dorion Sagan, *What Is Life?* (Berkeley: University of California Press, 1995), 30.

3   Dennis Tenen, "Distributed Agency in the Novel," Forthcoming in: *New Literary History* 53, no. 4, Autumn (Baltimore: Johns Hopkins University Press, 2022/2023): 903–7.

4   Emily M. Bender, Timnit Gebru, Angelina McMillan-Major, and Shmargaret Shmitchell, "On the Dangers of Stochastic Parrots: Can Language Models Be Too Big?," *FAccT '21: Proceedings of the 2021 ACM Conference on Fairness, Accountability, and Transparency*, March (2021): 610–23, https://doi.org/10.1145/3442188.3445922 (accessed April 13, 2023).

5   N. Katherine Hayles, "Inside the Mind of an AI: Materiality and the Crisis of Representation." In: New Literary History 53, no. 4, Autumn (Baltimore: Johns Hopkins University Press, 2022/2023): 635–66.

4

Good Technology Is Earthly

Rosi Braidotti

Eleanor was hooked on Rosi's philosophy from the first time she watched her mesmerize a lecture hall on YouTube. In the flesh, Rosi embodies her own lively, life-oriented or "vitalist" philosophy, speaking with a momentum and energy that makes it impossible to think about anything else. It's no surprise that she is one of the foremost continental philosophers alive today and has a vast global following. When Eleanor finally got to meet her in Bologna in 2017, it seemed Rosi would be one of the last successful stars of the Humanities, which would soon be replaced with digital or computational modes of research. But today, the Humanities are still very much thriving—even Google has to employ linguists to make its language models. As she describes in this essay, Rosi's 'posthumanism' is at odds with "transhumanism," the dominant way of thinking about what it means to be human—or more than human—in the age of AI. Feminism is foundational to the way she thinks about how invasive, pervasive technologies affect the people we have now become. Feminism asks that we uphold relationships with our existing bodies and Earth, rather than abandoning ship for other interplanetary colonial endeavors.

I am very much a technophilic person. There was never a moment where humanoids didn't use sticks and stones and other devices to get by—animals do it too, by the way. I love technologies and I think there have been long traditions in both feminism and traditional cultures of technology proving liberatory to women and other marginalized people. But with its Leftist political leanings, European feminism has a difficult relationship to technologies and robots. The Luddite rebellions, when textile workers rebelled against automation in the nineteenth century, were symptomatic of this. Automation and robotics are still seen as potentially hostile to human labor, and especially to the categories of humans that are marginalized as sexualized and racialized others: women, LBGT+ people, Indigenous, Black, colonized people, and the nonhuman world. Technology has the potential to make their fate even worse.

Thinking with the idea of the good robot, we need to confront the fact that technology has been grafted onto a culture that dehumanizes or considers some of us not fully human. We are not all human in the same way and to the same extent. As a nonhuman, the good robot is potentially closer to dehumanized and marginalized (sexualized and racialized) humans. This means that it can be a friend and an ally, as shown explicitly in feminist science fiction and Afrofuturism. But the robot is also the product of scientific rationality and advanced capitalism, and so it can be antagonistic to feminist values. This can produce a creative tension in feminist, anti-racist, and anti-fascist cultures, which contrasts with the hostile position historically taken up by the Left on technology. I see contemporary feminism as correcting that and trying to move a step further. Good robots are possible, but some negotiations are necessary.

Gendered identities and sexuality are never absent from the social history of technologies. Bodies and technologies interact in different ways depending on the historical moment. In my book *Metamorphosis*, I reflect on the cyber feminism of the 1990s as a hopeful euphoria for technology, which then dissipates into critical techno-doom.[1] Further back in history, early twentieth-century classic films like *Metropolis* illuminated this duplicity.[2] It shows the good robot Maria leading the revolution of humanity, but also threatening its future at the same time. What struck me about this ambivalence is that it shows to what extent technology was already sexualized and gendered. Technology very much operates within the gender system. The feminine both directs the future of humanity and exceeds scientific reason.

Today gender and technology have a different relationship. Contemporary capitalism is defined by invasive, immersive, all-pervasive technologies that are a lot closer to us, literally in our ears and eyes. There are no clear partitions or demarcations between the human and the technological other. This is *not* a dualistic system of clear oppositions, but rather one that blurs boundaries and complicates our relationship to the idea of the good robot. It replaces sexual difference as a binary with a multiplication of a thousand little sexes, legal genders, nomadic sexualities. This is the disruptive, even revolutionary potential of new technologies. Posthuman feminism, like Biohacking, Xenofeminism, transfeminism, or Gaga Feminism—as Jack Halberstam calls it—explores the liberatory potential of immersive technologies that also explode the gender system. That's an incredible and exciting prospect. The problem is that a transgressive multiplication of genders does not happen in a vacuum but in a world where we are still governed by the gender system. Dividing humanity into two genders makes it really manageable: you can divide and conquer forever. This means that advanced capitalism simultaneously undoes the gender binary and reinstates it.

We see this clearly in the transhumanist project of Elon Musk. He has funded multiple ways of moving beyond the human through his neural enhancement firm and the exploration of Mars with SpaceX and other private enterprises, and has invested billions into NASA. He aims to colonize outer space by 2026, with the first human colony on the moon to serve as a relay for the Mars station. And who is Musk going to send out there? A man and a woman. So there is a reinscription of the classical gender binary even while new technology holds the possibility of exploding the gender system.

Non-binary
New technology holds the possibility of exploding the gender system.

For me that tension is a defining feature of posthumanism, which I define as the convergence of advanced technologies with very fast environmental degradation, thereby grounding the whole project of redefining the human. Transhumanist capitalism exploits the paradoxes of humanity and transposes them to the posthuman era. We run the risk of new colonizations in space replicating the worst features of terrestrial patriarchy and capitalism. That's a bad science fiction scenario and we feminists can write better ones. We see this reactive trend in the image of Leonardo da Vinci's Vitruvian Man on the patch worn by NASA astronauts on their suits. The Renaissance idea of Man by da Vinci is still *the* image of humanity on Earth and now in outer space. With its perfect proportions defined by the architectural golden mean, it is also beautiful—there is no question about that. But it is a masculinist, ableist, and Eurocentric image of the human, and it excludes enormous swathes of humans. "The human" is a term that indexes exclusions. Humanism is a hierarchical system that defines the human in terms of all those that do not match the norm, including the sexualized, racialized, or naturalized others that I mentioned before.

It is significant that the exclusionary image of the Vitruvian Man is at the center of the transhumanist project, which unfortunately is the dominant way of thinking about what it means to be posthuman today. Its key players include Nick Bostrom at the University of Oxford and Elon Musk, or even Silicon Valley as a whole. This transhumanist movement has instilled the need for intrusive technological interventions upon our minds and bodies, redefining the very boundaries and meaning of the human, as well as human relationships to technology. Practices of human enhancement are now quite common, for instance in medicine and healthcare, but also in AI and industrial applications. The ethos of advanced capitalism is human enhancement and the transhumanists defend it as a neo-humanist way of perfecting the human. In so doing, they argue that they accomplish the Enlightenment project of humans evolving through science and technology.

Enhancement is supposed to bridge the gap between humans and computational systems that are way faster than human neural systems. Its research projects are, significantly, called "superintelligence" and "Human+." Some evolutionary logic is clearly being used here. But we are evolving socially anyway—just watch young children today playing computer games and you will acknowledge that they are a different species from my generation. Enforced evolution is full of pitfalls and challenges, but it is ongoing. I don't see why we need expensive transhumanist enhancement projects to accelerate it even further. As a gay woman, a feminist committed to social justice and transformative politics, I am slightly concerned about who gets to be enhanced, through what means, and for what purpose. My concern is that many people who are not considered fully human are excluded from the enhancement project, as is the environment. My critical posthumanism stands against this dominant ideology of transhumanism.

May Elon Musk go to Mars, with his transhumanist programme, but back on Earth, we have a planet that is depleted by climate change and social inequalities. Musk is ruthless when he talks about planet Earth, saying that it has exhausted all resources, so human life must continue elsewhere. The exploration of Mars is about mining and bringing down resources, and when Donald Trump was the president he passed an international law, which Joe Biden confirmed, allowing mining on other planets. This is not science fiction; it's advanced capitalism gone intergalactic. I remain concerned about this planet and would like a commitment to the sustainability of life on Earth for the Earthlings, as opposed to the transhumanists who are already abandoning the old planetary model. My critical posthumanism stands against that dominant ideology of transhumanism. It worries me that they are prepared to sacrifice the Earth and those who must stay here. While there is an old debate in cyberfeminism over whether we are proud to be flesh or whether we want to be cyborg, it is a problem that being proud to be just anthropomorphically human is out of the question for transhumanists. And we are never in fact "just human." The body is always embedded with nonhumans, whether organic—bacteria, animals, and plants— or technological—algorithms, codes, and networks. Thinking about all of that is a bit of a headache. But we need to rise to the complexity of what we have made possible. We cannot think in antiquated terms about what we have now become.

The way human autonomy is discussed today in relation to technology needs to catch up to this. The terminology and the idea of autonomy is highly disputed, especially in French philosophy, and yet it is as integral a part of dominant legal and moral systems as it is to the work of great liberal feminists like Martha Nussbaum.[3] I respect but do not share their premise. In continental philosophy, we emphasize relationships to multiple other entities rather than separations from them, and we call this a relational ethics. There's a whole tradition of posthuman feminism from Jane Bennett and N. Katherine Hayles to Donna Haraway that reshapes and repurposes the idea of autonomy.[4] I can't say that it rejects it, because it looks carefully at both what autonomy can contribute and what it excludes. The idea of autonomy that we critique comes from the European Enlightenment, which upheld Immanuel Kant's principles of Man's transcendental rationality, consciousness, and inbuilt moral compass. This triad of moral goodness, reason, and beauty defines the Enlightened man as a unitary and autonomous subject and it justifies the exclusion of multiple others. This is why feminists criticized it. But autonomy has also become a distinctive feature of liberalism that sees individualism as the key to emancipation and freedom. Its proponents run from John Stuart Mill to Gloria Steinem and Hillary Clinton. However, I have always argued that liberal individualism's model of citizenship is exclusionary. Historically, it left women, LBGTQ+ people, Jewish, and Black and Indigenous people out of the picture.

With each advanced technology we ask, "Who are we?" But really, every time we ask that question, do we have to go back to debunked eighteenth-century ideas about the human? Can we not be attuned to our complexities? I would say it's a task for the Humanities to evolve beyond a museum of old ideas and develop language and terminology to describe ourselves that deals with this complexity within the grammatical structures that we've inherited from the past. Grammar expresses who we are politically. The hierarchies of being are embedded in language, so we must evolve conceptually. We can't fall back on humanist language and imagery because we don't resemble the Vitruvian Man by any standard: that was a long time ago and a lot has happened since. We need a more creative idea of what we're capable of becoming that is generative and affirmative—but critical too. We need nondeterministic philosophies of life to deal with what is happening to our environment. Good robots are fine, but not if they impact our planet and the Earthlings negatively.

Notes

1. Rosi Braidotti, *Metamorphosis: Towards a Materialist Theory of Becoming* (Cambridge: Polity, 2002).

2. Fritz Lang, dir. *Metropolis*, Universum Film A.G. (UFA), 1927.

3. Martha Nussbaum, *Cultivating Humanity* (Cambridge, MA: Harvard University Press, 1999).

4. Jane Bennett, *Vibrant Matter: A Political Ecology of Things* (Durham: Duke University Press 2010); N. Katherine Hayles, *How We Became Posthuman* (Durham: Duke University Press, 1999); Donna Haraway, *Making Kin in the Chthulucene* (Durham: Duke University Press, 2016).

5

Good Technology Is Intergenerational

Sneha Revanur

About two or three years ago, I came across an investigation into an algorithm called COMPAS, an AI-powered pretrial system used to evaluate whether a defendant is at risk of committing further crimes in the time between their arrest and their sentencing. That was my first encounter with algorithmic injustice and my first awakening to the existence of AI bias. What I found out through that investigation was that COMPAS's algorithm was twice as likely to rate Black defendants as high risk even when they weren't actually going to commit future crimes.[1] The fact that the disparity was by a factor of two really woke me up to this reality of how while we often perceive technology as perfectly scientific, objective, and neutral, in reality it is actually amplifying, encoding, and perpetuating existing systems of oppression. This is seen in criminal justice, health care, education, hiring, housing, and many other sectors of society where AI is used.

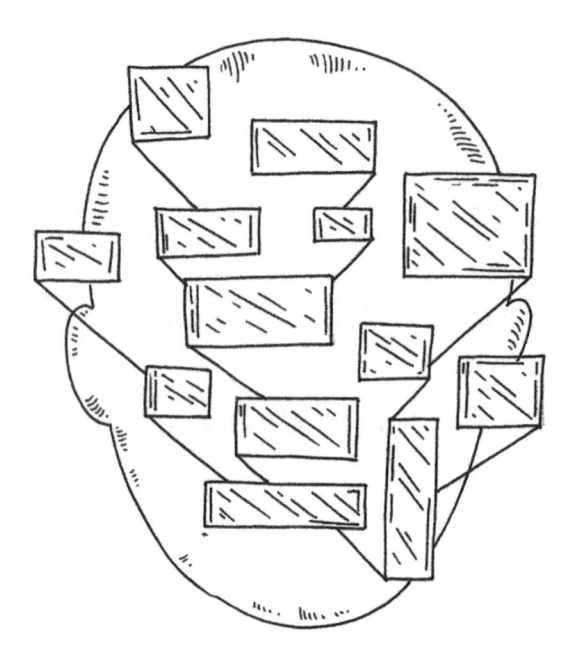

AI Bias
What I found out through that investigation was that COMPAS's algorithm was twice as likely to rate Black defendants as high risk even when they weren't actually going to commit future crimes.

Last summer, I found out that there was a ballot measure in my home state of California that would have expanded the use of the same kinds of algorithms in our home state.[2] I was outraged that there was not only almost no youth involvement in fighting the measure but also almost no organized pushback by Californian civil society. From there, I jumped into the scene and we formed Encode Justice. Encode Justice is an international grassroots movement of youth activists advocating for the ethical and human-centered use of AI. Our first initiative was focused on fighting that ballot measure, California Proposition 25. After dedicated organizing and changemaking we were able to eventually defeat the measure by a 13 percent margin.[3] That was a pretty energizing victory.

From there, I recognized that this problem is one that transcends California and the United States. It's a global humanitarian challenge for the twenty-first century that we are going to have to reckon with. I began to read more about other cases of algorithmic injustice, including those relating to facial recognition. We expanded to more states and more countries, and launched more campaigns. Even though young people are generally digitally literate there's little awareness of AI ethics issues. I think that when we talk about AI ethics, it is often a conversation reserved for people with PhDs and advanced academic backgrounds, even though the people who are actually the most impacted by algorithmic decisions are not those people. The general public is too often left out of those decision-making spaces where they could have some power and control over how algorithms govern their lives. This was what I first sought to dismantle. I also wanted to bring young people into the conversation because I had seen how we had risen up against climate change and gun violence. I wanted to recreate those mobilizations in our campaign for algorithmic justice.

Action
I wanted to recreate those mobilizations in our campaign for algorithmic justice.

Inaccessibility is the biggest barrier when it comes to youth getting into the AI space. We at Encode Justice are actively trying to combat that with our own curricular offerings, educational programs, workshops, events, materials, and things like that. Specifically, we have launched an AI ethics workshop program that prioritizes accessibility and sharing these stories and case studies of injustice. Our lesson plans span AI ethics and how algorithmic injustice affects health care, policing, hiring, and more. We have a pretty wide-ranging curriculum and we have been able to teach over 3000 students around the world directly in high school classrooms as well as at libraries, hackathons, conferences, and other venues. This has brought us a long way in terms of reaching underrepresented communities, specifically Black, Brown, and low-income communities. By sharing our knowledge of AI ethics with a wide range of participants, we aim to train the next generation of socially conscious developers and changemakers in AI ethics.

Because under-eighteens are the most digitally connected generation we have ever had, we are also the most predisposed to experiencing social media radicalization. Algorithms push people toward more and more extreme views that sometimes provoke feelings of hatred and inspire violence. Young people are the most vulnerable to experiencing the impact of those pipelines and falling down those rabbit holes. Young women of color are also the most vulnerable to experiencing feelings of inadequacy and low self-esteem because we're not well-represented in digital media. There's an archetypal social media persona that dominates TikTok, for example, a lighter-skinned, able-bodied person. Those standards definitely impose themselves and young people who don't fit those conventions are left feeling inadequate. So young people have had a unique experience, because we've spent our entire lifetimes with technology at our fingertips. We are less likely to see it as an entirely objective and neutral thing because we have directly experienced its impacts. We know how it pervades our everyday lives, shaping how we view ourselves, our confidence and self-esteem, how we view our friends and our communities, and whether we engage in certain actions, including violence. In that sense, there is definitely a reason to be optimistic about what Gen Z can achieve in response. I believe that young people will also enter the workforce as socially aware developers and technologists because we have that unique understanding of how technology shapes our worldview and interactions.

Consequently, I think a lot about how we can get more young people into office and into spaces of political power and decision-making rooms where they can ultimately shape how we think about and deploy algorithms. We can bring to the table this raw grassroots activist energy. We also have a unique ability to see discrimination and injustice through an intersectional lens. Youth activism has also been uniquely intersectional, as we have seen when young people came out in support of the Black Lives Matter movement. Intersectionality means that people experience different kinds of oppression. You might experience discrimination because of your age but also other factors like race, class, location, and gender. For example, when we talk about risk assessment algorithms, age is the single most predictive variable for those algorithms in determining what a defendant's risk score will be, followed by race and gender.[4] What that means is that these tools disproportionately penalize young men of color who are mythologized as superpredators, have experienced the school to prison pipeline, and endured decades and even centuries of racist injustices. Intersectionality is also a huge issue in the context of facial recognition technology, where a long-standing harmful myth associating Black women with masculinity has led to these tools confusing Black women with men. This explains Black women's staggeringly lower rates of accurate identification in facial recognition than any other group.

Because Black people are among the groups that are most susceptible to being misidentified, there have already been three wrongful arrests due to facial recognition technology in the United States. Arrests are a problem because they can quickly escalate to convictions and to fundamentally violating defendants' due process rights. When we get to that stage of AI nullifying due process and reshaping our judicial systems as we know them, that is a more dangerous reality. There have been many precursors of these kinds of racialized surveillance technologies, which is why I don't think future technologies will bring up harms that we haven't seen precursors to or aspects of. I think we are just going to be moving further and further down the pipeline. This for me is deeply troubling. But, we are fighting back. One of our campaigns at Encode Justice centers on banning the US government's use of facial recognition technology.

We can attribute the US government's reliance on these technologies to techno-chauvinism. It is a concept or an idea that expresses the false mentality that technology is somehow a panacea or silver bullet for all of our most pressing challenges. This is obviously a very misguided mindset. When we think about good technology, we have to break free from that mentality and recognize the misconceptions inherent to that. We should not approach the world from the mindset of AI or algorithms solving every problem when often they simply automate existing discrimination and re-institutionalize them, subsequently amplifying existing social hierarchies. We need to flip the script and break away from these conventions rather than simply re-automating them.

Because technology is not neutral, good technology must actively seek to counter existing hierarchies. It should not seek to operate within existing spaces; instead, it should seek to challenge those spaces. Good technology is specifically centered on achieving liberatory purposes. Young people want to see anti-racist technology and technology that is actively feminist or that actively tries to correct historical patterns of gender injustice. We want to see technologies that are cognizant of varying gender identities, such as people who are nonbinary and transgender. Technology operates on binaries that are currently unable to process the diversity of genders. That stifles the expression of identity. This is why we need to work toward technologies that can liberate people from those trends. They should be anti-racist, feminist, and actively uplifting for young people, people of color, and LGBTQ+ youth.

These technologies are possible and some of them exist right now. One example is a tool that rates the risk of US judges violating the Constitution or violating defendants' due process rights instead of rating the criminality of defendants. The Stanford Computational Policy Lab has also developed an automated race redaction tool that allows for more fair decisions to be made on criminal charges. A judicial risk assessment tool has also been developed by some of my amazing colleagues at the MIT Media Lab.[5] I think that these examples are very uplifting, liberatory uses of technology that not only actively counter and challenge existing hierarchies and systems but also center the people and affected communities in their development and their usage. I definitely consider these good technologies. And I do fundamentally have faith that we can move toward a reality in which these kinds of tools are more commonplace—in which they are, in fact, the standard for all technologies that we use.

This cannot happen without more and better intergenerational conversations. We have to convey to older people why we want to reshape AI by sharing our experiences and stories. Whenever I have conversations with older folks about algorithms and algorithmic justice, I make sure to cite the specific examples that young people are experiencing, from social media radicalization pipelines and risk assessment tools to facial recognition technology. I talk about how the algorithms that drive TikTok and other social media platforms actually reinforce existing beauty standards, influencing our perceptions of ourselves and our confidence levels. By contextualizing technology and our experiences of it in case studies and examples, I think that we're able to better communicate to other people who are not impacted by the same examples how it feels to be on the receiving end of those algorithmic harms and discriminations. I think that this is the best way that we can break down those barriers and facilitate more effective communication.

We need to do this with policymakers too, who often have the most power to shape technology regulation but the most surface-level understanding of how those technologies actually work. This inhibits effective regulation and good governance. The Band-Aid solution is to just get young people into the office and give us more space for political power. But in this day and age, we must facilitate intergenerational conversation by sharing our own experiences of algorithmic harm when we demonstrate the need for effective technology regulation in these areas. At Encode Justice we're also expanding our educational outreach initiatives to include older generations and make sure that we're able to make this content more accessible and digestible to them.[6] Ultimately, intergenerational cooperation will make the difference.

Notes

1 Julia Angwin, "Machine Bias," *ProPublica*, May 23, 2016, https://www.propublica.org/article/machine-bias-risk-assessments-in-criminal-sentencing.

2   Rachel Metz and Scottie Andrew, "In California, Voters Must Choose Between Cash Bail and Algorithms," *CNN*, October 31, 2020, https://edition.cnn.com/2020/10/31/tech/prop-25-cash-bail-algorithm-california/index.html.

3   Patrick McGreevy, "Prop. 25, Which Would Have Abolished California's Cash Bail System, Is Rejected by Voters," *Los Angeles Times*, November 3, 2020, https://www.latimes.com/california/story/2020-11-03/2020-california-election-prop-25-results.

4   "Age," *Pretrial Risk*, n.d., https://pretrialrisk.com/the-danger/demographic-bias/age/.

5   Evan Sernoffsky, "SF DA Gascón Launching Tool to Remove Race When Deciding to Charge Suspects," *SF Chronicle*, June 12, 2019, https://www.sfchronicle.com/crime/article/SF-DA-Gasc-n-launching-tool-to-remove-race-when-13971721.php#:~:text=San%20Francisco%20District%20Attorney%20George%20Gasc%C3%B3n%20on%20Wednesday%20said%20he,whether%20to%20criminally%20charge%20suspects.

6   Rebekah Agwunobi, Chelsea Barabas, Colin Doyle, and J. B. Rubinovitz, "Judicial Risk Assessment," *MIT Media Lab*, August 2020, https://www.media.mit.edu/projects/judicial-risk-assessment/overview/.

Part II

Good Systems

Kerry McInerney

In the past few years, we have seen numerous high-profile incidents of Big Tech fails, from AI hiring tools that discriminate against female candidates through to the racist and sexist labeling of images on platforms like ImageNet. Whenever these scandals occur, the guilty party tends to argue that this incident is a bug or an error in the system, one that needs to be quickly fixed in order to return the system to a state of neutrality. Similarly, when we experience discrimination along the lines of gender, sexuality, age, race, disability, and other axes of oppression, well-meaning bystanders often excuse these incidents as anomalies that are not at all representative of someone's character or an institution's culture. Alternatively, they argue that these harms are largely attributable to a small number of "bad apples" who can and should be removed from a system, leaving a healthy barrel of apples behind. Take, for example, the high-profile firing of the Google engineer James Damore for his anti-diversity manifesto, which suggested that the underrepresentation of women at Google was partially due to natural or biological differences between men and women. While Damore quickly became the face of sexism in the tech industry, the focus on his individual views obscures how misogyny more broadly underwrites Big Tech. But, as the feminist theorist Sara Ahmed argues, "the reduction of racism to the figure of 'the racist' allows structural or institutional forms of racism to recede from view, by projecting racism onto a figure that is easily discarded." Similarly, the reduction of racism and sexism in technological systems to a "bug" allows the larger systemic structures at play to recede from view.

Individual acts of racism and sexism are symptomatic of much deeper forms of systemic discrimination that underpin the fabric of our societies. This also runs true for the forms of harms and discrimination levied by technical systems. As one of our contributors in the last section, Jason Edward Lewis, writes: "the bias in these systems is not a bug but rather a feature of an interlocking set of knowledge systems designed over centuries to benefit white men first and foremost." This is particularly ironic given that new technologies are often positioned as the saviors that will solve the problems generated by racist and sexist systems of power. Contributors Wendy Hui Kyong Chun and hannah holtzclaw gesture toward this in their chapter when they write, "it is difficult to answer the question 'what is good technology?' because many of the crises we face stem from attempts to create good technologies, that is, technologies that will solve political, environmental, and social problems for us."

Hence, good technology should not be considered only a technical problem, but also a political and social one. Technical systems, like social and political systems, are not inherently neutral and they are not created in a vacuum. While new technologies are often celebrated for their innovative and novel properties, Black feminist scholars like Ruha Benjamin and Lelia Marie Hampton show how the underlying logics and ideas that shape many of these technologies are not as "new" as they appear. Rather than breaking from history, the so-called fourth Industrial Revolution of new technologies like AI form part of a *sociohistorical continuum* (a pattern, a chain) of power and control. For example, as Jennifer Lee explores in this part, technological advances offer novel ways of enacting much older forms of racial surveillance.

This part shows how technical systems are always entwined with the wider social and political systems within which they are developed and deployed. Breaking the sociohistorical continuum and creating good technical systems requires building better social, ethical and political ones. For example, as Jason Edward Lewis argues, in Big Tech companies that operate within a profit-driven capitalistic framework, a good system is merely one that generates the most profit. This might encourage designers to cut corners and produce products that do not work for everyone, leading to the high-profile technological failures I mentioned earlier. This is why contributor Soraj Hongladarom suggests in his chapter that good technology may be possible but there are conditions. He, like the other contributors in this section, presciently asks: "under what conditions can we make technology work better for us?"

6

Good Technology Is Inclusive

Margaret Mitchell

Margaret Mitchell is a trailblazer in the field of AI ethics, where she's led research on fairness, transparency, accountability, and bias in AI systems. She's proposed new ways of enforcing transparent model reporting, developed improved face attribute detection for gendered and racial minorities, spoken out against pseudoscience in AI, and pioneered leading research on the risks posed by large language models. In 2018, she became the founder of Google's Ethical AI team, where she led Google's most diverse team to date. Sadly, in 2020, Google abruptly fired Meg's Ethical AI co-lead Dr Timnit Gebru. Three months later, Meg was also fired. Their dismissals incited worldwide outrage and protest, and Google's behavior towards them quickly became a cautionary example about the limits of AI Ethics work within Big Tech organizations. It also became a flagship example of how pervasive sexism and racism shapes the AI industry. Despite this adversity, Meg continues to take delight from her intellectually rigorous computer science work, while also maintaining her down-to-earth and humorous nature when engaging in the fight against misogyny in AI.

Many who are working on issues of bias in technical systems, and their propensity to proliferate patterns of discrimination, are people who are minorities in technology development and experience these patterns themselves. They are people whose ideas are often *marginalized*, appropriated by others while the majority forgets their contributions. As they are left out of meetings or shared documents, their unique reflections are *erased*, as are the balance of priorities that comes from their experiences. The majority's impression of the minority is through the lens of *stereotypes*: the nuanced details of who each person are instead washed over with more familiar cultural caricatures.

People who "see" patterns of discrimination understand how critical it is not to propagate it. While you don't have to see discrimination in order to understand why it is critical to stop it in its tracks, part and parcel of systemic discrimination within the technology field is not doing anything meaningful about it—even when people experiencing it clearly explain what's happening. If a situation is fundamentally discriminatory, but the discrimination within it is not "seen" nor recognized by people in positions of power, then the next step of *addressing* that discrimination becomes unavailable.

It is critical to face the reality of systemic discrimination in tech, and its dynamics, to understand where we're currently situated as a society in creating "good" technology. In order to create "good" technology for tomorrow, we have to see a path there from where we are now. But where we are now leads down a path where people with characteristics that are not well-represented in technology are also the victims of *bad* technology.

To begin discussing good technology, here is a minimal notion of "good" that readers may mostly agree is one of many ideas about what a "good" future might look like: everything is the same, *except* that those currently on the lower end of power differentials—women, people of color, older people, disabled people are just some examples—have improved lives with respect to those differentials. They are less *marginalized*, or less stereotyped. This is a world that is more equitable—culturally, socioeconomically—than the current one. This is one where, for example, disabled people have the assistance they need to navigate spaces with the same ease as the abled people those spaces are most often built for. This is a world where women are promoted at the same rates as men, and women are not disproportionately subject to misogyny, hatred, sexualization, and violence. This is a world where women are well-represented in tech *before* Artificial General Intelligence (AGI) is declared to be solved.

In order to think through how we might get to something like this "good" kind of technology, we can ground our thinking on the current relationship between technology and people with characteristics on the lower end of power differentials. This relationship can be analyzed along two main axes: the technology itself and the culture supporting its development. For example, in current AI systems, some religions—such as Islam—are disproportionately associated with violence. In the surrounding technology culture, people of some age groups—such as those over fifty—are all but absent. This, in turn, affects what kinds of technology is created. Women are similarly poorly represented in technology and technology culture: Within artificially intelligent systems, women are sexualized (from revenge porn to MyReplika), objectified (as Abeba Birhane has shown), and subject to violence.[1] Within technological design and culture, women and nonbinary people are frequently excluded and alienated—while also being sexualized or objectified (or worse).[2]

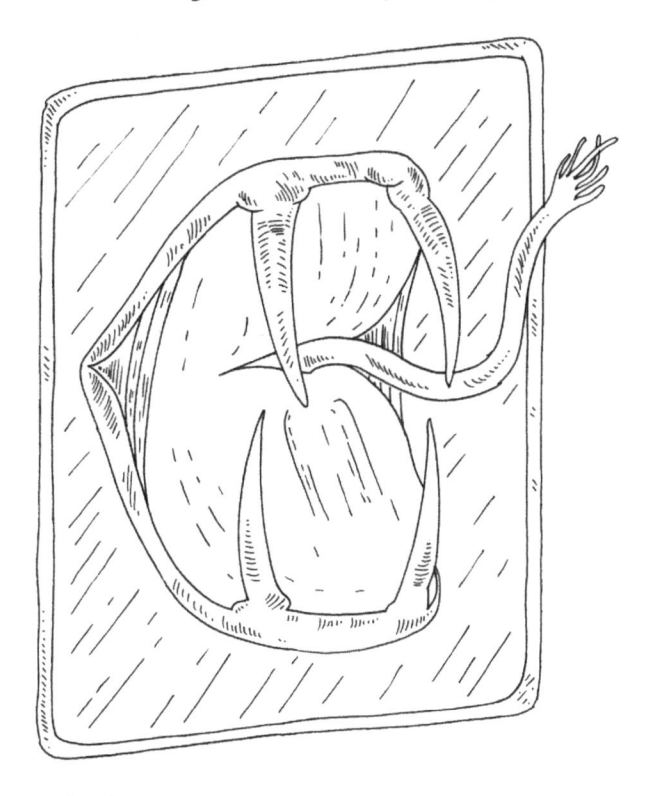

Dangerous Technology
Within technological design and culture, women and non-binary people are frequently excluded and alienated, while also being sexualized or objectified (or worse).

The reasons for gender alienation from AI systems stem in part from its sources. Datasets used to create these systems are based on data available on the web, such as text and images from social media sites, blogs, and wikis. Within these spaces, there are persistent and well-known practices of infantilization and sexualization of women, as Emma Kavanagh and Chelsea Litchfield have shown.[3] These beliefs are propagated by AI systems because they can only learn from past data: they cannot learn from data that is not yet there. And so the question of *whose history matters?* within the data used to train systems is a fundamental one. Similar to the saying, "histories are written by the victors," the stories and beliefs of people with characteristics that are subject to marginalization and historical harm are represented through the lens of the beneficiaries of the status quo. This is a lens of domination and reduction rather than a just representation of real lived experiences. Further, the reasons for gender alienation within AI culture are not fundamentally different from the reasons AI data is alienating: the majority sees, and treats, women as caricatures rather than real people.

Following the definition of "good" technology above, this technology paradigm is the opposite of what a "good" technology might create. Such a vast gulf cannot be bridged, especially as technology and the structural problems within its development proliferate: milestones for equality move farther away. We must therefore work to redefine the structures of technology, focusing on the creation of inclusive spaces and the incentivization of technology culture that empowers women and others on the lower end of power differentials.

Let's turn to a worked example of the disconnect between goals of equality and the state-of-the-art. Recently relevant in the AI landscape are Large Language Models (LLMs) and AGI. Briefly, language models underpin much of the language-based aspects of technology—everything from recommendations on your social media feed to autosuggest. In their most basic form, they are what makes AI able to "talk," producing words and phrases that we are able to get meaning from. Until very recently, it was easy to tell when you were talking to a language model versus a person. Now the lines are blurred: it is really difficult to tell. For many working in technology, this makes the goal of creating AGI—a system that is at least as intelligent as a person—appear obtainable.

The difficulty in distinguishing a person from a deployed LLM is a function of recent advancements. LLMs can now produce vast detail on topics (whether or not those details are correct), and somewhat coherent long-distance conversational structures. The vast detail is based on the problematic data discussed above. The advancement in conversational abilities refers to how a topic at the start of a conversation can be more or less appropriately referenced again later on in the conversation. That is, when people are having a conversation, we generally have a sense of the topics discussed and can have embedded conversations within conversations as we drift between topics and pop back up to topics mentioned earlier. Language models never exhibited this behavior before, but now they are beginning to. The "short-term" memory of language models has generally been one of the real tells for whether it's human or not, and that tell is rapidly vanishing.

These capabilities have created a renewed interest in AGI but not a corresponding interest in equitable data (or culture) practices to create that intelligence. This can be contrasted with work on task-based intelligence, which focuses on defining specific tasks that a system could do to help, augment, or assist someone—key behaviors for engendering equality—and the kind of data needed to achieve those goals. This might be, for example, a system that people who are blind can query to better access the visual world around them, or a system focused on helping immigrants to quickly communicate in the local language. But these kinds of task-specific assistive technologies are generally developed by people in minority positions within tech, and discussions on their importance are underrepresented in technology discourse. Instead, the vast majority focuses on creating something "intelligent" from discriminatory data, within discriminatory environments, ignoring (or "not seeing") the discriminatory aspects.

And so concerns around AI *replacing* people, rather than *assisting* people, are well-motivated alongside concerns about AI reifying discriminatory structures in society. By focusing on "general," human-like intelligence, rather than task-specific intelligence, and by doing so within discriminatory environments, we move far afield from creating mechanisms to bring about more equal access to opportunity and towards instead creating a being that's *sort of* in our own image, except constrained by the hegemonic and misogynistic views that proliferate in development culture and the data used to train it. Similarly, there is an argument to be made that building technology with goals of task-based assistance is preferable to building technology for general-purpose replacements. But this is barely part of the conversation as increasingly human-like systems proliferate on discriminatory data without a clear definition of the tasks they serve nor how helpful they are for humankind.

There are clear solutions for working toward "good" technology from a feminist perspective, within technology development as well as outside of it. Within, there must be recognition from the majority that women (and other non-men) are marginalized. This is currently not recognized in practice, and there are no cultural norms for how *not* to marginalize women. Norms that would fundamentally change the system include the following:

1. **Diversity norms:** Paying attention to "who is in the room": If a meeting is more than two people, and they are all men, there is a problem. To address this, each time there is a meeting, sharing of documents, or anything else that includes more than one person, it's critical to think through who the people who aren't men involved with the project are. It may take a second; for each person who is thought of, there will be a pull to think they don't play a role that's relevant for the discussion: this is systemic discrimination in action.

2. **Relevance norms:** Related to above, the very fundamental question of *who is relevant?* in different technology discussions and spaces is one that needs to be redefined in order to proactively address systemic discrimination. This requires recognizing the women who are qualified on a topic within technology development, and inviting those women to share their perspectives on different projects and decisions.

3. **Inclusion norms:** This means incorporating the perspectives of qualified women and nonbinary people into what should be developed or how it should be shared publicly. Complementary to diversity norms, inclusion norms focus on making sure people with marginalized characteristics *feel welcome* to share their views. Amplify their ideas, attributed to them. Say their names in meetings and reference their good work.

Outside of direct technology development, people can turn the approach in AI toward values-focused paradigms by paying persistent attention to the interaction between technology and human rights. For example, journalists must continue to report on the experiences of people affected by technology, including reporting on how current technology takes away from, rather than improves, the livelihood of people. Insightful reporting from journalists such as Karen Hao and Khari Johnson has highlighted how colonialist exploitation practices influence how modern AI systems are trained, and how deployed systems lead to a loss of rights for people with minority characteristics (e.g., Uyghurs in China).[4] More of this type of reporting, rather than bedazzled AI hype (often coming from people with less marginalized characteristics), can help to beat a constant drum reminding the general public as well as developers what AI technology is, how to understand it, and the larger picture of what it means to use it. One simple solution for the general public is to read these pieces, and subscribe to (i.e., pay for) the journalistic content.

Changing the approach in AI technology also requires that the general public demand a future where the technology provides for more equal access to opportunity. Such technology could take many forms, everything from systems that monitor and help correct implicit biases of management to systems that diversify the kinds of content we're exposed to online in order to be as inclusive as possible. We must demand technology that helps us, rather than dazzles us, from from tech companies, their funders, and our representatives. We need increased transparency in technology, accountability from those who create it, and the inclusion of diverse voices.

As final thoughts: We can imagine what "good" technology might look like, and articulate likely paths to get there, yet the path we are on does not show clear signs of leading to technology that is good. On the contrary, we appear to be on a path where for women, nonbinary individuals, and others with characteristics that are commonly marginalized in society—particularly Western white society—technology will only further exacerbate historic inequality. But by prioritizing *inclusion* as the most fundamental problem to solve within technology, we can create a path forward for good technology to flourish.

Path
The path we are on does not show clear signs of leading to technology that is good.

Notes

1   Karen Hao, "Deepfake Porn Is Ruining Women's Lives. Now the Law May Finally Ban It," *Technology Review*, 2021, https://www.technologyreview.com/2021/02/12/1018222/deepfake-revenge-porn-coming-ban/; Jessica M. Goldstein, "Revenge Porn Was Already Commonplace. The Pandemic Has Made it Worse," *Washington Post*, 2020, https://www.washingtonpost.com/lifestyle/style/revenge-porn-nonconsensual-porn/2020/10/28/603b88f4-dbf1-11ea-b205-ff838e15a9a6_story.html; Ashley Bardharn, "Men Are Creating AI Girlfriends and Then Verbally Abusing Them," *Futurism*, 2022, https://futurism.com/chatbot-abuse; "Incident 266: Replika's 'AI Companions' Reportedly Abused by Its Users," AI Incident Database, 2022, https://incidentdatabase.ai/cite/266/; Abeba Birhane, Vinay Uday Prabhu, and Emmanuel Kahembwe, "Multimodal Datasets: Misogyny, Pornography, and Malignant Stereotypes,"

Computers and Society (2021), arXiv:2110.01963v1; Mairead Eastin Moloney and Tony P. Love, "Assessing Online Misogyny: Perspectives from Sociology and Feminist Media Studies," *Sociology Compass* 12, no. 5 (2018): e12125577, https://doi.org/10.1111/soc4.77.

2   Katta Spiel, Os Keyes, and Pınar Barlas, "Patching Gender: Non-binary Utopias in HCI," in *Extended Abstracts of the 2019 CHI Conference on Human Factors in Computing Systems (CHI EA 'f19)*. Association for Computing Machinery, New York, Paper alt05, 2019, 1–11.

3   Emma J. Kavanagh, Chelsea Litchfield, and Jaquelyn Osborne, "Sporting Women and Social Media: Sexualization, Misogyny and Gender Based Violence in Online Spaces," *International Journal of Sport Communication* 12, no. 4 (2019): 552–72, https://doi.org/10.1123/ijsc.2019-0079.

4   Karen Hao, "Artificial Intelligence Is Creating a New Colonial World Order," *MIT Technology Review*, 2022, https://www.technologyreview.com/2022/04/19/1049592/artificial-intelligence-colonialism/; Khari Johnson, "Iran Says Face Recognition Will ID Women Breaking Hijab Laws," *WIRED*, 2023; Khari Johnson, "DeepMind Researchers Propose Rebuilding the AI Industry on a Base of Anticolonialism," *VentureBeat*, July 2020, https://www.technologyreview.com/2022/04/19/1049592/artificial-intelligence-colonialism/.

7

Good Technology Is Possible—But There Are Conditions

Soraj Hongladarom

When we first came across Soraj's work on Buddhist approaches to computer ethics there was already a lot of excitement around what Eastern spiritual and religious traditions could do in technology. Of course, there are many ways of practicing Buddhism, and many more of applying it to AI contexts. We were excited by how much more radical the Buddhist principle of non-malfeasance (do no harm) is than the tech industry's weaker invocation to "not be biased." We were also struck by Soraj's take on "machine enlightenment," by which he aims beyond "good technology" to enlightened technology. What would it take to create a machine that was enlightened?, he asked. There are many paths to enlightenment, and Soraj's vision of it is compatible and complementary to other forms of ethics, notably feminism. He believes that feminism is a way of working toward social inclusion for the marginalized, which fits with Buddhism's goal that no one in society should be neglected.

Technology is what defines us as humans. The Neanderthals used certain kinds of technologies such as stone tools to help them survive the harsh Ice Age for hundreds of thousands of years, and we *Homo sapiens* have developed technology into the sophisticated forms we find it in today. So whether it is good or bad we have lived with technology for as long as our species has existed.

However, many of the technologies that are with us today are a far cry from those developed by early *Homo sapiens* or the Neanderthals. Now talk about technology totally replacing us does not sound as fantastical as it seemed only a few decades ago. The more news that we hear about the latest achievements of technology, the more tangible that possibility becomes.

This possibility of technology becoming so powerful as to make us eventually redundant has prompted this question: Is good technology possible? The question sounds a bit like "Are good politicians possible?" For a large number of people, good politicians are not possible because they are disillusioned with them. However, in a democratic society, it is not possible to live without politicians, so instead of asking whether good politicians are possible, we should ask instead under what conditions do politicians become better. That is, we need laws and institutions that are designed to regulate their behavior and ensure that they are accountable.

The same, I argue, is true for technology. Since we cannot live without technology, the question needs to become: Under what conditions can we make technology work better for us? Thus, technology can become good if certain conditions are obtained. And I would like to show that there are three such conditions. These are: (1) technology must be beneficial, (2) the ethical dimension must be ingrained in the design and conceptualization of technology, and (3) there must be a higher-order theory of the goodness of technology that helps us fully realize the first two conditions.

That technology must be beneficial and must produce benefits to us human beings should go without question. This is the reason our species designed technology, beginning with fire and stone tools, in the first place. However, the question of whether technology is really good mostly centers on benefits. Are the benefits that technology is supposed to bring really beneficial? What if the positives go to only certain groups of people, creating inequality? And what about the situation where one type of technology brings in certain benefits, only to create harm in other areas?

These are difficult questions that cannot be answered in this short chapter. Perhaps we could follow the utilitarians and try to balance the benefits and harms as if all were commensurable, or perhaps we don't have to. The idea is to create benefits through technology in such a way that the harms are minimized.

This is necessarily an ongoing process. New harms are created all the time, especially when new technologies are introduced. The harms associated with today's AI technologies are well-known; most importantly AI could exacerbate our already unequal society, making it even worse. Nonetheless, the benefits are there too. In order for AI to be a good technology, we need strongly concerted efforts to eliminate the harms and focus on the benefits. We must ensure that the benefits are shared by all sectors of humanity. This, moreover, is only a starting point and is not enough. An effort needs to be in place to ensure that those who are traditionally disadvantaged—women, minority groups, people in the Global South, and so on—receive the benefits of AI technology.

Buddhist thought can help us understand why we need to focus on equal sharing of benefits. The principle of compassion tells us that all beings are interconnected. This means that the suffering of others is essentially our own, and helping others become free from suffering means we are free from our own suffering too. If AI can indeed bring us benefits, these benefits must accrue to all groups equally.

For example, AI research and development can be done in such a way that women are more empowered. This is needed especially in the Global South, where women have suffered from millennia of inequality. Loan application apps, for instance, can be redesigned so that women receive more loans than they used to. In Thailand, women have traditionally participated significantly in local economic activities. AI can help them in many ways, such as providing them with the information that they need for their businesses; it can coordinate information from individual women in a particular area and create an overview picture of the situation for policymakers to make appropriate decisions.

The examples above lead to the second condition, which is that the design and implementation of technology such as AI must involve ethical considerations from the beginning. Developers cannot focus entirely on the functionality and efficiency of their products. In fact, functionality and efficiency would mean nothing if the ethical dimension is neglected. Functionality—what the technology is designed *for*—already contains values, and it is only a short move from this functional value to the ethical one. An AI algorithm might be designed to spot patterns in a large array of data and make predictions based on those patterns. These predictions are not only mathematical in form but they correspond to real-world conditions because the data fed into the algorithm come from the real world and represent real people and their activities. The functional value of the technology, therefore, cannot be limited only to enhancing the power or profits of only certain groups; otherwise it will lead to a violation of the principle of compassion alluded to earlier.

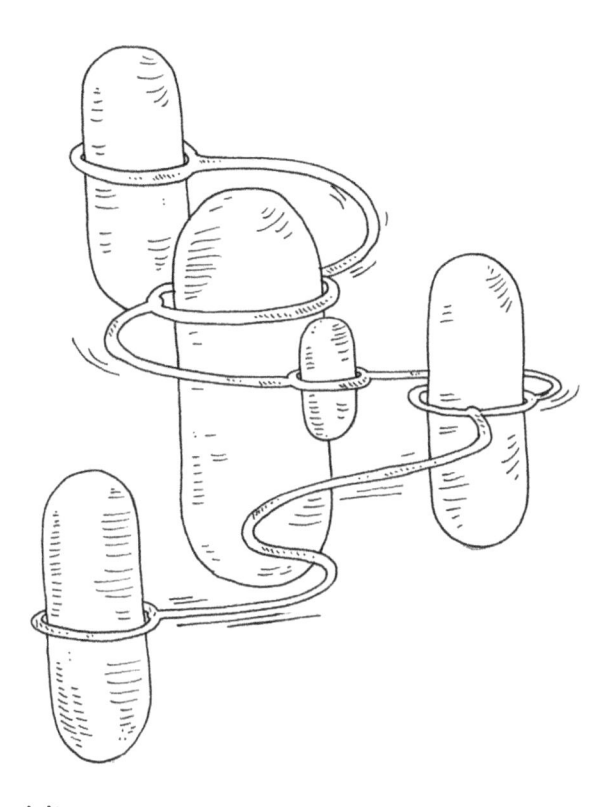

Interconnectivity
The principle of compassion tells us that all beings are interconnected.

Hence, the design of AI must be such that care for these neglected values—care for women, children, minorities, and so on—become integral to the functional values for which the algorithm is designed in the first place. This implies that the dataset fed into the machine learning algorithm must be modified if the modification will result in more women being included in the design rather than otherwise. This does not have to mean that the data set does not represent reality. If reality is such that women are excluded, then modification of the data set so as to create a more equal and inclusive society would be all for the better. Technology can be better than what it is, and this is not a call for more efficient handling of functionality, which is obvious. Still, it is a call for technologists and engineers to pay more attention to the kinds of values that hitherto have been neglected. AI does not always have to be a tool for those who want to perpetuate the status quo, but I believe that it has the potential of transforming the world, not only physically but ethically and politically too.

The third condition for technology, especially AI, to be good is that there must be an appropriate way of conceptualizing the whole process. Here I would like to propose that Buddhist philosophy can offer a solution. What distinguishes the Buddhist theory from the standard ethical theory in the West is that it focuses on the idea that the ethical is what is in accordance with nature. This is also an ancient idea in Greek philosophy, which finds a lot of resonance with Buddhism. The idea is that there is a natural goal, which is the condition for real happiness for each and every human being, and what is good is just what leads us to eventually realize that goal. Thus, if technology can lead us to this natural goal, then this must be a condition for the technology to be good.

This idea comes from a very common truth that every human being, indeed every sentient being, desires happiness rather than suffering. Aristotle also says roughly the same thing, when he opens his *Nicomachean Ethics* as follows: "Every skill and every inquiry, and similarly every action and rational choice, is thought to aim at some good" (1094a).[1] This is not saying that all we want is pleasure because much pleasure at one time can lead to pain afterward. Pleasure in itself is not the same as happiness because sensitivity to pleasure can wane over time. On the contrary, it means that, ultimately, the kind of happiness that we naturally want must be the kind that results from cultivating one's own self and one's own practice. This is what constitutes the good.

Furthermore, the kind of happiness that Buddhism advocates cannot be fully achieved for certain individuals alone. Since everyone is connected with everyone else, we cannot achieve our own goals without depending in some way on others. This implies that social considerations play a significant role in Buddhist thought. Cultivating ourselves in this way implies pursuing the intention and action to help others also. This basis of Buddhist compassion, then, can be the source of motivation for the kind of social action and mechanism that ensures that AI does create social good that provides tangible benefits for everyone.

An objection to the Buddhist theory that I have sketched here is that what is good for someone is not necessarily good for others, and when these goods conflict then the theory seems to have a hard time deciding what should be done. However, the good that is the end result of our natural search for happiness is not the same as the immediate good that satisfies our desire at a moment in time. It is true that if there is only one television in the same room, one person's preference can indeed come into conflict with another's.

But for Buddhism, this is only the satisfaction of temporary desires. When you cultivate yourself, you realize that these satisfactions do not provide lasting happiness, and it is this lasting happiness that can be achieved by everyone at the same time without any conflict.

The issue is how to achieve that state, and in our context, the point then becomes how to design and implement systems that regulate technology so that that technology itself contributes to bringing about such a realization.

Enlightened
It is this lasting happiness that can be achieved by everyone at the same time without any conflict.

In the end, then, what we need is the kind of technology that contributes tangibly and concretely to the kind of society that is ethical, one that embraces traditionally excluded groups. We need more research and development of AI and autonomous systems that are not only friendly to women but also ones that are designed from the ground up with the aim of empowering them as well as redressing the millennia of oppression. AI developers must see what constitutes suffering in human society and design their products to fight against that. Equally important is that the developers must take a broader view of "suffering," and I have proposed that this broader vision can be achieved with Buddhist philosophy and a certain amount of Buddhist-related practice.

If these conditions that I have outlined so far are obtained, then good technology is indeed possible. And since these conditions are not too far-fetched so as to be impracticable—everything only depends on each of us, the conclusion in fact is that good technology is likely.

Note

1 Aristotle, *Nicomachean Ethics,* trans. and ed. Roger Crisp (Cambridge: Cambridge University Press, 2004), 3.

8

Good Technology Is Community-Centric

Jennifer Lee

Kerry first met Jen at Cambridge, where she was doing her Masters in Public Policy. They quickly bonded over their shared love of acroyoga (which combines yoga with acrobatics). Fast-forward a few years, and Kerry and Jen reconnected over a very different interest: Jen's incredible work at the American Civil Liberties Union of Washington (ACLU-WA). Along with Silicon Valley and Seattle, Washington is one of the heartlands of Big Tech in the United States. Despite this, King County, Washington, was the first county in the United States to ban facial recognition technology. This, we believe, can partially be attributed to the incredible campaigning work of Jen and the ACLU-WA. She continues to fight tirelessly for privacy rights and better tech ecosystems led from below by those who are most likely to be negatively impacted by technology.

When we seek to designate technology as "good" or "bad" it is important to ask: Who gets to define what "good" in "good technology" means? Who gets to define the "costs" and "benefits" of a specific technology, and who has the power to decide whether a technology is a net positive or a negative for our collective societal well-being?

In my role leading the technology policy work at the American Civil Liberties Union of Washington, I have observed that decisions about a technology's utility, design, and deployment are often made without meaningful input from community members who are most at risk of harm from that technology. Even when there are community engagement processes in place, these procedures can result in the co-opting of community voices and the legitimization of decisions that have already been made. These decisions often minimize the surveillance risks posed by technologies, while amplifying a narrative that technology will create convenience for all or serve as an easy panacea for much deeper societal issues.

For example, in 2019, the Port of Seattle instituted a partial moratorium on the use of biometrics at Seattle-Tacoma International Airport. The ACLU of Washington, alongside a number of other organizations dedicated to protecting people's rights and civil liberties, served on a working group called the Biometrics External Advisory Group and urged the Port to reject collaboration with US Customs and Border Protection (CBP), a sister agency of Immigration and Customs Enforcement (ICE). Despite our many calls for the Port to reject participation in CBP's mass collection of biometric data, Port Commissioners voted to authorize a $5.7 million Request for Proposal to procure and implement a "shared-use" facial recognition system, partly to increase efficiencies at the Port. Despite the Port spending millions of its own dollars to help advance federal biometric surveillance, it declared that it had effectively banned biometric surveillance and implemented "tangible, enforceable policies" "with the help of a Biometrics External Advisory Group." It seemed that the Port had made a decision to move forward with working with CBP from the outset; the RFP had been published even before the advisory group had made its recommendation.

Recognizing that there are institutional and sociocultural power assumptions at play in the decision to build, design, and deploy any technology helps us understand that "good technology" is deeply contextual and can only be subjective. The technologies we see around us today—both rudimentary and advanced—are disproportionately reflective of the value choices made by people in positions of privilege and power. These value choices inevitably shape the design, deployment, and regulation of technologies that frequently replicate and entrench power imbalances in favor of those who have historically wielded the most power.

Some may argue that technology is purely a neutral tool—that it is simply an instrument used to perform functions, and that it is these functions, rather than the technology, that should be deemed "good" or "bad" in certain contexts.[1] After all, a knife can be used to murder an individual, but it can also be used to remove a life-threatening tumor. However, the argument that technology is neutral is flawed because it does not consider that the motivation to build a certain technology and the technology's inherent design are always embedded with power-laden values. These values engineer and perpetuate a dominant culture that is by default considered good by decision-makers.

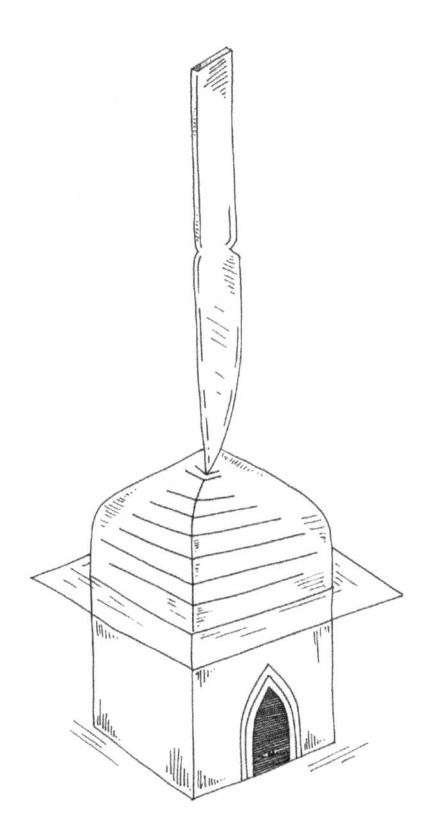

Surveillance
Surveillance technology has long been used by those in power to control and monitor those most vulnerable, whether or not the technology was originally designed for that purpose.

Values exist within all the objects and technologies we build around us. For example, slanted and segmented benches, bolts installed on steps, boulders under bridges, and fences around grates are not simply neutral design features in our cities, but rather, they are clear examples of hostile architecture purposely designed to prevent people experiencing homelessness from existing in public spaces.[2] As Robert Rosenberger describes in his book, *Callous Objects: Designs Against the Homeless*, curved benches prevent people sleeping on them and metal spikes stop them sitting on steps.[3] Similarly, boulders under bridges prevent people from taking shelter from rain or snow, while fences on grates in cities prevent people from huddling around or sleeping on top of them for warmth. When we examine the reason behind these designs, we can see the hostility towards homelessness embedded within them.

This type of architecture may be designated as "good" by those who have the power to maintain and perpetuate this design—by city government planners, individuals who do not wish to witness homelessness, or people who simply like the aesthetics of the design. But these design choices serve to perpetuate anti-homeless values and further stigmatize a vulnerable population, whether or not such values are explicitly named in the design and deployment process.

We can see how key drivers of technological development shape the values that are embedded in technology's design and function. For example, the government, and specifically, the military, is a critical driver of many innovations originally designed for the purpose of warfare.[4] Military organizations often fund, develop, and deploy technologies to exercise power and control over others, even if the same technologies are later used for different purposes that the public may see as "good."

In 2018, the US Army awarded Microsoft a $479 million contract that included the acquisition of 100,000 HoloLens augmented reality headsets to be used in both training and active battlefield situations. After that decision was made, 100 Microsoft employees wrote an open letter to the CEO and president of Microsoft demanding that Microsoft cancel its contract with the military, stating that they did not sign up to develop weapons of war. But that contract was not canceled, and in March of 2021, Microsoft won a new $22 billion contract to provide the military with this technology.

Victims of war, those subjected to military surveillance, and even some employees who built this technology may define it as harmful. However, those most susceptible to harm from it do not have as much power as corporate leadership and the US military to shape the cultural discourse around its impacts before it becomes widely deployed and accepted outside of military contexts. Even if a technology's original design and function would be considered widely harmful by the general public, often concerns about harm are neutralized by decision-makers who seek to legitimize a technology's use by broadening it for use in different sectors. There are certainly applications of augmented reality headsets that many individuals would probably define as "good." It is easier to consider an augmented reality headset a "good technology" when we associate it with learning in the classroom or enjoyment of a game; it is more difficult to do so when we consider that the tool was purposely built for warfare and when we live in a country under the occupation of a military that uses those headsets as training tools to kill.

A technology may be considered good or of little impact for a group of people, while simultaneously being massively harmful for other groups. For example, Israeli military and surveillance technology is often developed for and tested on Palestinians living under military occupation, but is rejected for use on Israeli citizens. Facial recognition is used to scan Palestinians at checkpoints, but proposals by law enforcement to install facial recognition cameras in public spaces in Israel were rejected; similarly, NSO Pegasus surveillance software is used by Israeli police to infiltrate Palestinians'" phones, but such use on Israeli citizens was widely debated and condemned.[5] Even though there is recognition from the dominant group in this context that these tools would be harmful if used on them, this technology is allowed to be used on Palestinians who do not have power in decisions regarding the deployment and regulation of these technologies.

Additionally, technologies that disproportionately harm marginalized groups create collective societal harms that may not be easily visible to dominant groups, such as the erosion of privacy rights and other civil liberties. For example, the use of location tracking via surveillance technologies like automated license plate readers or ALPRs, which are used for law and parking enforcement and traffic management purposes, may seem innocuous.

But ALPR technology has been a key tool long used by law enforcement to conduct dragnet surveillance of innocent members of the public. After 9/11, the New York Police Department used ALPR technology to illegally target the Muslim community for over a decade. The NYPD mapped where members of the Muslim community lived, stationed ALPR-equipped cars outside of mosques, and tracked worshippers attending services, placing the names of thousands of innocent New Yorkers in secret police files.[6] And while this surveillance program was ultimately struck down as illegal, it placed unwarranted stigma and suspicion on the Muslim community, made people fear openly practicing their religion or even appearing religious, created community fear, and chilled free speech. These are harms that still resonate today.

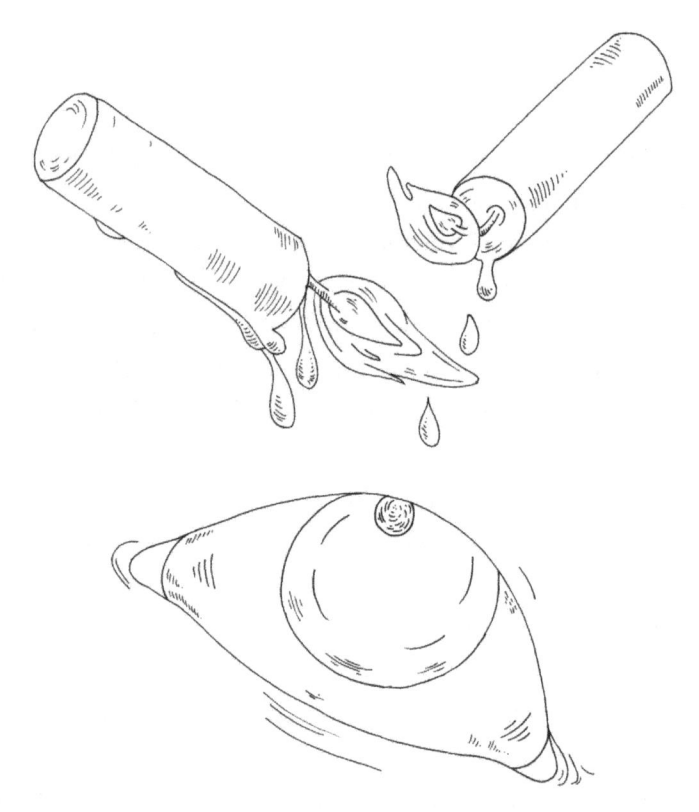

Lantern Laws
Lantern Laws were an early form of surveillance that incentivized and made it possible for white people to enforce slave systems and incarceration.

This technology often has few limitations on its use and can be used to track where people live, work, practice their religion, seek health care, and participate in public demonstrations. Police officers have used ALPR databases to search for romantic interests;[7] to blackmail owners of cars near a gay bar;[8] and to surveil immigrants for deportation.[9] Widespread use of such technology certainly harms groups already under disproportionate scrutiny by law enforcement, but it also chills democratic rights for everyone.

If we want to build, deploy, and regulate technology to be "good," not just for those who hold the most privilege and power in our society, but rather for communities who are often harmed by technology, it is critical to examine the long history of surveillance. Surveillance technology has long been used by those in power to control and monitor those most vulnerable, whether or not the technology was originally designed for that purpose. For example, after the Slave Revolts in 1712, in 1713, New York City passed what were called "Lantern Laws" requiring only Black, mixed-race, and Indigenous people to illuminate themselves by carrying a lit candle at night—the technology of the time.

Lantern Laws were an early form of surveillance that incentivized and made it possible for white people to enforce slave systems and incarceration. As Simone Browne explains in her book *Dark Matters*, Lantern Laws were an early form of stop and frisk policing that deputized any white person to stop those who walked without the lit candle after dark.[10]

As technologies have advanced, the same institutions that have always caused harm are now equipped with tools truly unprecedented in their surveillance power, such as facial recognition, location tracking, drones, and AI-based tools. While many technologies are specifically developed to surveil marginalized communities, even technologies that are developed and deployed ostensibly for innocuous purposes can reinforce white supremacy and exacerbate power abuses at every level.

We can see a parallel to Lantern Laws in the city of San Diego's installation and use of smart city streetlights. In 2016, San Diego installed energy-saving LEDs, cameras, and sensors, supposedly for sustainability and city planning purposes. These streetlights were intended to record public space 24/7 in high definition in order to provide the city with traffic data, including parking spot detection and pedestrian analysis. But after the murder of George Floyd in

2020, it was revealed that the San Diego police were surveilling Black Lives Matter protesters using the smart city streetlight footage. They continuously used the streetlights to surveil and arrest protesters. Soon after the height of the protests, the city turned off the stream of transit and mobility data, and these street lights officially became an exclusive tool for local police. According to *Voice of San Diego*, the city had paid for many of these lights with grants intended to "help local communities overcome poverty" so the city had justified the installation of the streetlights by putting most of them in "low- to moderate-income neighborhoods."[11] This attempt to "help communities overcome poverty" actually had the effect of concentrating control in the same actors and institutions that reinforce racism and xenophobia, rather than in any transformative models of community power.

As Catherine D'Ignazio and Lauren Klein discuss in their book *Data Feminism*, we should be asking questions about whose interests are centered in conversations about data and technology.[12] Who gets to decide whether a technology is "good," who gets to define its harm, and who gets to ultimately decide if and how a technology is built, used, and regulated? If we are looking to build technology that is good for those who have been and continue to be most marginalized in our society, we need to be asking whether technologies advance equity from intersectional anti-racist, feminist, and decolonial perspectives, rather than from dominant, white supremacist norms. A technology's existence, design, purpose, and regulation needs to be fashioned with direction from those who have been historically disempowered. Otherwise, technology will undoubtedly serve to reinforce the status quo and perpetuate existing structural inequities. It is important to note that designing and regulating technology to protect the rights and liberties of those most vulnerable will help protect everyone's collective rights and liberties.

Our work in Washington with the Tech Equity Coalition, a group of organizations and individuals that aims to center historically marginalized communities in decisions about technology, has enabled us to push back against some of the dominant assumptions about technology. In 2020, we passed the first multi-city county ban on facial recognition in the United States in King County, Washington, home of the headquarters of Big Tech giants, Amazon and Microsoft. In 2022, we advocated with community members to successfully fight back against a $1 million budget allocation for gunshot detection systems, such as ShotSpotter, which has been proven to be ineffective at preventing or investigating gun violence while imposing serious surveillance risks. For four years in a row, we defeated a weak, industry-backed data privacy bill that would have set a ceiling for privacy protections. In 2023, we passed the My Health My Data Act, a first-of-its-kind privacy law in the United States that protects consumer health data, including period-tracking app and geolocation data, which have been used to track and target people seeking reproductive and gender-affirming care.

Creating technology that is good for equity requires both individual action and systems-level change. Individually, we need to focus on changing power structures within the different contexts in which we operate, by questioning the norms and assumptions inherent in decisions on if and how to build, deploy, and regulate technologies. We all have a responsibility to urge the institutions in which we work to cede decision-making authority to marginalized voices, and to share our power with those who have less. Collectively, we need to organize to tackle the interlinked systems that legitimize and perpetuate existing harmful power structures. Whether we are addressing corporate capture in academia and government, changing exclusionary policy-making spaces, altering legal systems, or challenging power structures in nonprofits, companies, educational spaces, and government entities, we should be asking, what would it look like for impacted community members to actually drive decisions about technology and take leadership in defining what good technology means for them?

Notes

1 Douglas Allchin, "Thinking about Technology and the Technology of 'Thinking About,'" *Techné: Research in Philosophy and Technology* 5, no. 1 (2000): n.d., https://scholar.lib.vt.edu/ejournals/SPT/v5n1/allchin.html.

2 Jennifer Lee, "Power and Technology: Who Gets to Make the Decisions?" *Interactions* 28, no. 1 (2021): 38–46.

3 Robert Rosenberger, *Callous Objects: Designs against the Homeless* (Minneapolis: University of Minnesota Press, 2017).

4 Patrick Lin, "Robots, Ethics & War," *The Center for Internet and Society at Stanford Law School*, https://cyberlaw.stanford.edu/blog/2010/12/robots-ethics-war (accessed December 15, 2010).

5 Jalal Abukhater, "Under Israeli Surveillance: Living in Dystopia, in Palestine," *Aljazeera*, https://www.aljazeera.com/opinions/2022/4/13/under-israeli-surveillance-living-in-dystopia-in-palestine (accessed April 13, 2022).

6 NYCLU, "Raza v. City of New York (Challenging the NYPD's Muslim Surveillance Program)," New York Civil Liberties Union, https://www.nyclu.org/en/cases/raza-v-city-new-york-challenging-nypds-muslim-surveillance-program (accessed n.d.).

7 Melanie Ehrenkranz, "Cop Used Police Database to Creep on Over 100 Women, Investigation Finds," *Gizmodo*, https://gizmodo.com/cop-uses-police-database-to-creep-on-over-100-women-in-1833156806 (accessed March 8, 2019).

8 Julia Angwin and Jennifer Valentino-DeVries, "New Tracking Frontier: Your License Plates," *The Wall Street Journal*, https://www.wsj.com/articles/SB10000872396390443995604578004723603576296 (accessed September 29, 2012).

9 Vasudha Talla, "Documents Reveal ICE Using Driver Location Data from Local Police for Deportations," *American Civil Liberties Union*, https://www.aclu.org/news/immigrants-rights/documents-reveal-ice-using-driver-location-data (accessed March 13, 2019).

10 Simone Browne, *On the Surveillance of Blackness* (Durham: Duke University Press, 2015).

11 Jesse Marx, "Years into Smart Streetlights Program, Council Will Write Surveillance Rules," *Voice of San Diego*, https://voiceofsandiego.org/2020/07/09/years-into-smart-streetlights-program-council-will-write-surveillance-rules/ (accessed July 9, 2020).

12 Catherine D'Ignazio and Lauren Klein, "1. The Power Chapter," in *Data Feminism* (Cambridge, MA: The MIT Press, 2020), https://data-feminism.mitpress.mit.edu/pub/vi8obxh7.

9

Good Technology Is Participatory

David Adelani

David is one of those people that makes community projects happen. Managing teams of volunteers is no easy feat, and it takes a visionary like David to spur everyone along. Throughout his busy computer science PhD he also volunteered at Masakhane, a grassroots organization that is trying to improve Natural Language Processing (which powers Search, translation, and many other online tools) for over 2000 African languages. While the computer science community often tries to do new things without a good reason why, David's publications are oriented towards solving real problems: How can we make this tool work in low-resource scenarios? How can we create a uniquely African speech corpus for language models? How can pre-trained models perform better on African languages? We see these efforts toward making a world that is more inclusive as a distinctly feminist ambition, as is the way David goes about it: kindly and collaboratively.

In 2020 I joined Masakhane, a grassroots organization whose mission is to strengthen and support natural language processing (NLP) research in African languages. Masakhane's work is for Africans and by Africans. There is a real emphasis on work being done by African researchers—of course with the support of like-minded people around the world. Masakhane is an isiZuluword which means "we build together." That is what has been happening in our participatory research. It's a really inclusive community made up of people from different disciplines, like linguists, technologists, policymakers, computer researchers, and scientists, and we are working together but based across the globe. I am very glad that the founders of the group are women, because this has really encouraged many women to join us and feel welcome in the group. Women are leading amazing projects in Masakhane; in fact, they lead most of our biggest projects.

Masakhane has two main goals. The first is to tackle underrepresentation by getting more AI scientists across Africa to be involved in building AI datasets and models. The second is to increase research on African languages. Africa is very linguistically diverse—it has over 2000 languages, and on average each is spoken by a large number of people. It is really important that all of these languages are represented by AI. Until recently, most AI evaluations of African languages were only based on Swahili, but Nigeria alone has over 500 languages, and many of them have different linguistic characteristics. Currently very few machine translation tools support African languages. The nonavailability of these tools for Africa is a big problem; after all, we take it for granted that European languages are widely supported by AI tools.

At Masakhane we are making sure we're not just working on dominant African languages but those with fewer numbers of speakers, as well as endangered languages. Most people who work for Masakhane are English speakers and so we are really keen to encourage people who come from or speak the languages of Francophone Africa, Portuguese Africa, and Arabic parts of North Africa to join us. Ideally we want a spread of people from across the continent: West, East, Central, South, and North. We are also taking data from interesting sources that are more representative of the kinds of everyday texts people interact with, like notebooks, prayer books, proverbial books, and cookery books. These are also accessible forms of language that make it easier for the people who do not speak English and who have not had access to as much education to join us.

Many people who have tried to work on African languages in the past have not done this and have taken languages from nonrepresentative sources.[1] This is not the right way to go about data collection and model training for these languages. Another major issue is that native speakers are often not consulted at all. Companies have just crawled the web, taking conversations off social media and scraping Wikipedia pages.[2] And where native speakers are involved in the process, they are rarely compensated properly or acknowledged in publications.

The other major problem with building natural language processing capabilities for African languages is finding funding. Industry entrepreneurs are very skeptical about investing in African languages because it is unclear what their market value will be. Without being able to predict and measure their economic benefits, funders are not incentivized to invest in African language technologies. But it is incredibly important to the people who speak these languages that they do. We need more investment in education, mentorship, and collaborative work, as well as internships with top labs and AI companies. Masakhane is trying to do its part to contribute to this by inviting researchers from around the world to collaborate with African researchers and native language speakers. This is also helping to close the global knowledge gap in AI, which is another huge barrier to good technology. Africans cannot solve the problem if we do not have the skills. It is important that those skills are not just in the possession of people from one area of Africa but are shared by people across the continent. For example, if you have made a technology that is meant to be rolled out across Africa and it works better for Bantu languages but less well for West African languages, it is more likely that someone recognizes this in design phases if West African language speakers are part of the process.

The Masakhane community is combating siloes in AI knowledge across Africa by increasing the diversity and volume of its members. We already have more than 400 members from 30 African countries. Being part of such a dispersed grassroots organization brings its own joys and challenges.

We Build Together
Being part of such a dispersed grassroots organization brings its own joys and challenges.

First, the members are amazing to work with. When you see the enthusiasm, energy, and passion that people have for African languages—even collaborators who don't speak the languages—it is truly amazing. It also makes me incredibly happy how fast and easy it is to scale projects to include many languages. For example, when I wanted to build a named entity-recognition dataset for Yoruba, my native language, I shared the idea with Masakhane in our weekly meeting and a lot of people expressed an interest in it: they said that they too wanted to do the same thing for their languages. It was a beautiful thing to see how straightforward it was to scale a project from one to twenty languages. This was made even easier by the fact that all our work is open source. Open source is important to us because we want to share knowledge and build an inclusive community. In practice, this means that when you start a project everyone can see what you are doing and help out.

There are of course challenges to doing AI research with so many people. The major one is keeping volunteers motivated when working on a voluntary basis. For example, the process of building the named-entity recognition system for African languages was labor intensive. It required a new dataset that we called the MasakhaNER dataset, and more than forty annotators were involved in building it. During that time I kept asking myself, how do I keep motivating them, encouraging them? I sent a ton of messages to the people who spoke the relevant languages saying, keep going, let's do this, we've got this. Sometimes you have to give extra time and host extra weekly meetings to assist them in the annotation, even though you are not even a speaker of the language. It is time consuming but worth it. Why would I not give my time when there are people who are spending more than ten or twenty hours a week doing this work? By contrast I am only being asked to spare thirty minutes of my time, so it is my pleasure to do this gladly. I have learned that one of the best ways to keep morale high and motivate people is to set a deadline for an international conference or workshop, and let contributors know they are going to be part of a paper. They need to see their efforts acknowledged. Making them feel respected and part of something that's recognized by the research community for being important challenges people to really work hard even when they are not being paid for it.

Last year we submitted a paper to the African NLP workshop and the Empirical Methods in Natural Language Processing conference that combated a really important issue.[3] Most AI technologies need large amounts of data, but a team of us was looking into how we can build AI using less data. This is a really interesting direction and one that can help natural language processing for African languages because we lack data—digitized or online texts for different languages. We call this a low-resource scenario. Our work showed that it is possible to only use 10 to 100 data examples and still improve technologies like named-entity recognition. This is when you get AI to tag the same category of items or entities in text (like colors, shapes, or people). We've tested this on Hausa and Yoruba languages, and now we're working on this data shortage problem in other ways, for example, in relation to distant supervision. Distant supervision makes use of heuristics, rules, and online knowledge bases to label data in a (semi-)automatic way. This is used to automatically label entities in text data, for example. In order to do this automatic labeling, we first need native speakers to write simple rules. These are small, small, simple, simple ideas that you can integrate in situations where you don't have large amounts of data. You still get a very impressive performance, which shows that big data isn't always necessary.

We are also building models that work in places that don't have expensive AI infrastructure. Technologists need to bear in mind that most labs in Africa cannot afford all computer technologies. This is really important; people building technologies need to think really carefully about whether their tools can actually have an impact in places that can't use graphics processing units—electronic circuits that display graphics and other visual items on an electronic device—to power their AI. This might result in these labs not being able to run some AI programs at all, making many products as good as useless. That's why we're building machine translation models that work on a central processing unit, which is the bit of a computer that gives and takes instructions. We can do this without having the capacity of big companies like Google and Microsoft, and still make tools available in many African languages. Finally, we're also building solutions that can help address some of the Sustainable Development Goals on health, food security, and education in Africa. We're encouraging Africans to understand these issues and partake in finding solutions with us.

Masakhane will keep expanding—we'll be a force on the continent that can really change things. We are a good technology, because we help create technologies that improve people's quality of life without harming any group of people, and that work well in the places they are intended to be used.

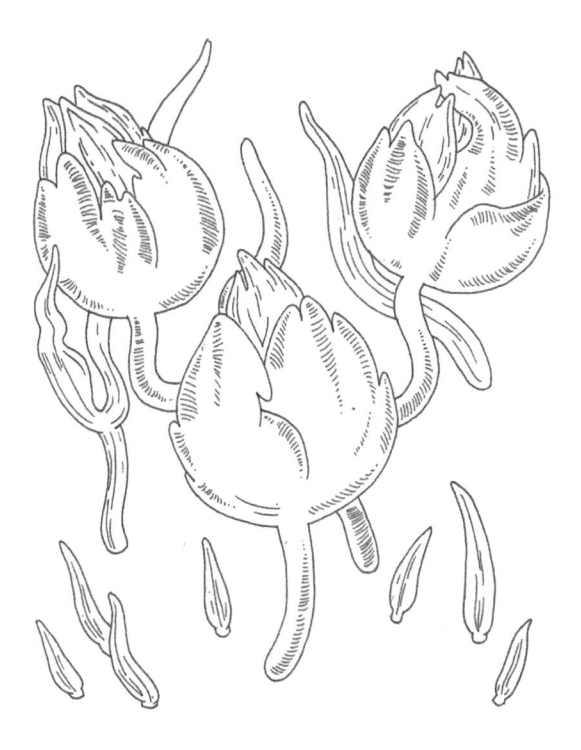

Gentle Growth
We are a good technology, because we help create technologies that improve people's quality of life without harming any group of people, and that work well in the places they are intended to be used.

Not all technologies can be easily regarded as a good technology, especially if they only work on some groups of people and are biased toward others, like facial recognition tools that have the worst accuracy for Black women while having an excellent performance for white males. It took the intervention of Black female researchers to protest its use for commercial purposes and surveillance before such products were abandoned[4]. Indeed, there may be some useful products that can be based on this technology, but until it supports all target groups, it is difficult to regard it as a good technology. We are careful about these issues while building language technologies for African languages, as we want technologies that support a diverse set of languages across Africa, including speech and language technologies that work for the old, young, male, female, and different speech accents. We're already spurring NLP research in African universities, but we do less research in Africa than the rest of the world. We now need to also encourage entrepreneurs to build solutions that work on indigenous African languages. Hopefully this will lead to economic prosperity on the continent. I think if Masakhane can achieve this—a full end-to-end system from research to industry that has a real impact on the life of Africans—then Africa will do amazing things. There are challenges, but organizations like Masakhane show that they are surmountable.

Notes

1. Wilhelmina Nekoto et al., "Participatory Research for Low-resourced Machine Translation: A Case Study in African Languages," in *Findings of the Association for Computational Linguistics: EMNLP 2020*, 2020, 2144–60, Online. Association for Computational Linguistics.

2. Yacine Jernite et al., "Data Governance in the Age of Large-Scale Data-Driven Language Technology," in *2022 ACM Conference on Fairness, Accountability, and Transparency (FAccT '22)* (New York: Association for Computing Machinery, 2022), 2206–22, https://doi.org/10.1145/3531146.3534637.

3. Michael A. Hedderich, David Adelani, Dawei Zhu, Jesujoba Alabi, Udia Markus, and Dietrich Klakow, "Transfer Learning and Distant Supervision for Multilingual Transformer Models: A Study on African Languages," in *Proceedings of the 2020 Conference on Empirical Methods in Natural Language Processing (EMNLP)*, 2020, 2580–91, Online. Association for Computational Linguistics.

4. Buolamwini, J. and T. Gebru, "Gender Shades: Intersectional Accuracy Disparities in Commercial Gender Classification." *Proceedings of Machine Learning Research* 81 (2018): 1–15, Conference on Fairness, Accountability, and Transparency.

Part III

Good Design

Kerry McInerney

The problem with good design is that it is easiest to identify when it is absent. You might have experienced this when trying to park your car in a badly signposted carpark or using a glitchy, unfriendly website. Bad design leaves us frustrated and angry. Good design, on the other hand, rarely draws praise. Too often, good design can be found in silence: in the moments where everything works as it should. Crucially, though, the infuriating moments when technology does not work illuminate who these technologies were designed *by* and *for* in the first place. The design theorist Sasha Costanza-Chock highlights how designers often work with a single universal user in mind when they make and test new products. However, the rich breadth and depth of human experiences and needs cannot be condensed down into a single ideal user. This means that when designers imagine a particular user in mind, they tend to imagine someone very much like themselves. In the relatively homogeneous and (unfortunately) not very diverse Western tech industry, this means that the "universal user" tends to be young, white, male, and able-bodied.

The exclusions indexed by this supposedly "universal" user result in tangible harm to those who fall outside of this narrow mold. Take, for example, smart home technologies that are used to track, control, and abuse intimate partners because designers have not considered the security risks posed by these products; voice recognition technologies that cannot make out different accents; and, as contributor David Adelani examines, natural language processing (NLP) technologies that do not incorporate a diverse array of languages. As Adelani's chapter shows, bad design is not just a question of user enjoyment or experience. Instead, it is a question of justice—or, as Costanza-Chock puts it, "design justice."

As disability theorists like Meryl Alper demonstrate, we need to create technologies that make worlds we can all fairly and freely inhabit. Designs are not merely outlines of what a product should look like and how it should function. Instead, they are far more encompassing *blueprints* of how we should live with and through technology, as well as how we should live with one another. Technology design reveals the complex and interlocking sets of values that we hold about technologies and their place in society. They also demonstrate the designers' worldviews, beliefs, and ideologies about the people who are using these products. Existing technologies reveal a narrow set of virtues deemed emblematic of good or well-designed technology, including efficiency, rationality, objectivity, profitability, and accuracy. Yet the contributors to this part ask, what if good design means creating technology that ascribes to other values? For example, in their chapter, Os Keyes asks, what if good technology means designing technology that is open and vulnerable rather than closed and invulnerable?

In this part, "design" functions as both a noun and a verb. It refers to the blueprints for the material products made by tech companies and the changes that must be made for these systems to be inclusive, positive and beneficial for everyone. For Priya Goswami, this includes design features like an "emergency exit" that allows users to "pull the plug" if a technology fails to work. Yet it also gestures toward the *processes, actions,* and *mindsets* that are required to design something well. For Ranjit Singh, this means fundamentally rejecting the "move fast and break things" mindset of Silicon Valley and instead embracing slowness in the technology development process. The contributors in this part therefore show how making good technology is a challenging and continuous process: one that is always in motion.

10

Good Technology Is Vulnerable

Os Keyes

Os is an incredible scholar, writer, and teacher, whose work spans everything from the problems with gender recognition technology through to how dehumanizing tropes about autism are encoded into AI. Their critique of recent work to improve AI's ability to recognize the faces of Black women is kind, generous, and uncompromising, as all good critical work should be. Hanging out with Os means delight and chaos in equal measure. They manage to get away with using relatively strong language and searingly humorous graphics in their writing through striking the right balance between academic irreverence and personableness; little wonder they're popular with both Vice *and the top journals in the field. Funny, humble, and completely dedicated to their students, Os is the person we all wish we had been taught by. Our podcast episode with Os still has the most intellectual variety of any episode we've ever recorded, so it is unsurprising that they have also edited hundreds of Wikipedia articles. Whenever we chat with Os we always learn something new from their outstanding breadth of knowledge, wisdom, and generosity, and this is present throughout their contribution to this volume.*

At first glance, arguing that technology is, or should be, vulnerable comes off as somewhere between incoherent and irresponsible. Incoherent because—with the exception of software vulnerabilities that can be exploited by hackers—vulnerability is more associated with people than things. Irresponsible because—as that exception suggests—most people think of vulnerability as a *bad* thing. As nothing more than being at risk of harm.

My view is that both of these understandings and reactions are wrong—that vulnerability and technology look nothing like this portrayal. A more accurate framing treats vulnerability not as the capacity to be harmed but as the capacity to *be moved*: to adapt, to shift, to flow. This capacity is essential to a feminist approach to technology design. The question then becomes this: If we use that understanding of vulnerability, how does that change our approach to technology?

Vulnerability
The capacity to be moved; to adapt, to shift, to flow.

We exist in what sociologists call "high modernity" (or postmodernity), one characteristic of which is an obsession with classification and perfection. In how it structures the design of technology (and the minds of technologists) modernity idealizes order and purity, and often (as a consequence) the *universal deployment* of fixed artifacts that make claims to perfection. In the artifacts that are produced in such environments, there is a strong tendency toward fixity—toward forms that try to preclude the involvement of users or other parties in shaping them. A prominent example is, of all things, tractors, specifically tractors designed by John Deere. In an effort to prevent user maintenance and modification, John Deere's lawyers have gone so far as to sue customers who have the temerity to tinker with their own tractor.[1] They are hardly alone in taking this approach: Apple, too, has structured the physical design of its phones (and the policies around licensing repair programs) to control as much as possible how devices are used, to the point of using proprietary screws in their phones just to make it as difficult as possible for them to be opened. In both of these examples, there is a clear motivation of *profit*; if technology cannot be repaired by the user, it has to be repaired by the designer, or replaced entirely, and in both cases the company extracts a fee.[2]

Of course, systems of order themselves are (as John Law puts it) "never complete. Instead they are more or less precarious and partial accomplishments that may be overturned."[3] And as we will see, in many places (including technology), users disrupt and discombobulate attempts to enforce order, despite the best efforts of developers. The example of John Deere tractors is so publicized precisely because users are campaigning to be allowed to modify their vehicles as they see fit. But that does not change the centrality of the *desire* for order and invulnerability, and the way that designs stemming from this desire shape that discombobulation.

What, then, is the alternative? I would argue it is technology designed around *vulnerability*. To many people, the idea of applying vulnerability as a concept to technology seems nonsensical: it is usually characterized as both specific to humans, and as largely a bad thing. Correspondingly, discussions of vulnerability and technology usually take the form of "how is this technology making us vulnerable?," by which the authors mean "how is this technology opening us up to harm?" A good example is Mark Coeckelbergh's "Human Being @ Risk,"[4] which treats the risk of vulnerability as inherently negative. But vulnerability is more than openness to harm; it is openness to change, good or bad. Vulnerable technology is thus technology designed, as Erinn Gilson would put it, to display "a basic kind of openness to being affected and affecting" by others.[5] Technology that users, and reusers, can change, adapt, and adjust.

The canonical example of vulnerable technology is (in some respects) free and open-source software (FOSS). As the name suggests, FOSS is a software characterized by both being free to use and (just as importantly) carrying with it the source code—the ingredients and recipe used to make it. Correspondingly, users can not only use and deploy it freely but also *modify* it, and use and distribute those modified versions in turn. FOSS directly or indirectly underwrites most of the technical infrastructure one might use in computing, from the structure of the internet to the very operating system you use to access it. If you are reading this on or near an Apple computer, for example, you are right by a system that, although locked down and proprietary, is built on open-source code.

Of course, not all FOSS is the same; some comes with permission to reuse and redistribute it wherever the user sees fit, while other software restricts the user to avoiding (for example) commercial deployments. Openness to change and changeability is a spectrum, not a simple on or off. But designing technology to be vulnerable (or, at least, more vulnerable than it previously was), and making this vulnerability apparent to the user, opens up possibilities for adaptation. For different, plural orders, or things outside orders altogether.

This doesn't just apply to software but to physical technologies as well—just look at issues of repair. As the example of John Deere's tractors makes clear, a lot of hardware that we purchase is (sometimes intentionally) hard to repair and rework. As a consequence, it tends to get thrown away when it no longer fits what we need it to do. But some technologies are designed, as Daniela Rosner and collaborators have demonstrated,[6] *for* repair, or otherwise amenable to modification and improvement. The result has been the flourishing of spaces for repairing, hacking, and modifying everything from bicycles to IKEA furniture. Differently designed technologies, with different designerly emphases on fixity and invulnerability (or not), are more or less amenable to precisely this kind of work. Designing technology around vulnerability and flexibility would better enable spaces like this to flourish, and technology to be repurposed and improved rather than discarded. And as Kerry McInerney reminded me as we prepared this volume, adaptation is of central importance as we deal with a changing and increasingly unstable planet.

Looking at open-source software and repair also highlights some limits and difficulties. Just because you make something *technically* open does not mean you avoid issues of power. Scholars such as Judy Wajcman have been documenting, since the 1990s, how early feminist enthusiasm for the freedom and adaptability of the internet was rapidly crushed. The reason for this is, by and large, the people. Technologies, after all, are not just the "stuff": they are also the people and practices involved in designing and using it. For this reason, academics often speak not of "technical systems" but of "sociotechnical systems." And the socio- of sociotechnical systems—the people—are far less open to vulnerability, by and large, than the code. There are reasons for this that stretch beyond the individuals. At one level, we all live in a society that is intolerant of vulnerability: that treats it as something *bad*, and that valorizes invulnerability and (with it) the refusal to acknowledge failure, or the need for change.

But these attitudes are particularly magnified in engineering. The idea of perfection and invulnerability as the desired outcome of work runs deep, particularly in masculine cultures, and engineering is highly (albeit in some ways, atypically) masculine, as Christine Dunbar-Hester and Nathan Ensmenger have differently (but brilliantly) documented.[7] In many respects, engineering disciplines have made their reputation and obtained their social power by playing into this idea that they are full of unique, individualized geniuses. I once had a manager who opened her keynote at the company all-staff meeting with the line "programmers are wizards." Wizards, mavens, geniuses—our understanding of engineering is replete with these images of developers as uniquely skilled, and exclusively qualified, to shape technology, and has been for some time. So it's unsurprising that for people enculturated in this world, admitting the limits of one's work or understanding is often somewhere between unattractive and conceptually impossible.

The lesson here, though, is not to throw away the idea of vulnerable technology but to augment it—to return the focus, in part, to the people that make up technology, and ask how the cultures and practices and mindsets of technologists can change to make vulnerability meaningfully possible. There are some process-oriented changes that would help, like reworking the distance between developers and users. Much modern technology is developed through extended supply chains of many different parties—what the user encounters might be the output of a process with 300 different stages, and so the user's ability to address the people *behind* most of those stages is impeded (let alone those people's ability to relate to the user).[8] Shorter chains of relation would also make space for deeper and more vulnerable relationships between different parties to technology.

But much of what is needed is more interpersonal—more tacit. Specifically, it is changing our relationship to vulnerability: making it okay to be flawed, to be wrong, to adapt—to move. What would it look like for technologists, as Canadian philosopher Alexis Shotwell advocates more broadly,[9] to see personal insufficiency and failure, as well as technical bugs, as opportunities to do better? As signs of problems that need addressing, and engineering? What would it look like for our culture (as a field, and a society) to accept that, and to laud it? As odd as it might seem, inspiration can be found in approaches to restorative justice. Among other things, restorative justice is based on the premise that those responsible for harm are (or should be) in community with their victims, and that to harm is not, in and of itself, damning. Taken together, they emphasize the importance of responsible parties growing, and having space made for them to grow. They emphasize our shared responsibility, all of us, to enable that space. Perhaps, then, rather than changing what we make, or how we make it, part of the work of good technology is asking who we are, or are allowed to become, through the design of technology and the spaces in which that design takes place.

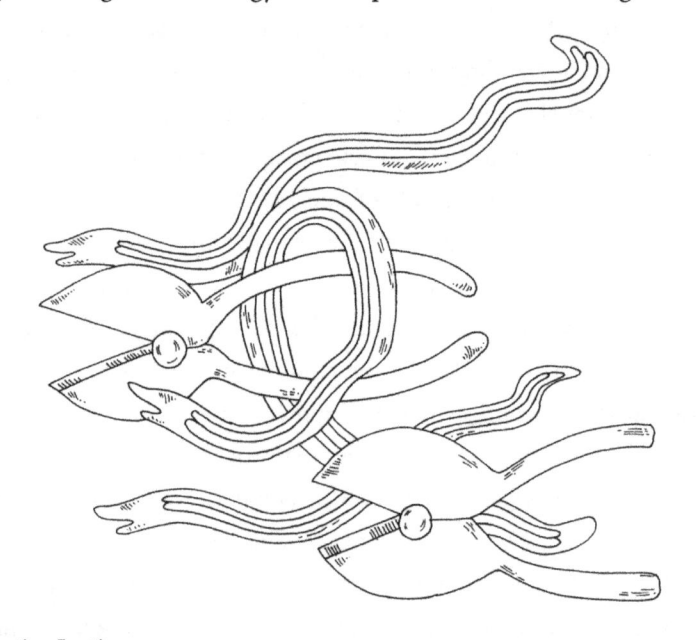

Restorative Justice
Those responsible for harm are (or should be) in community with their victims.

Like restorative justice, a call for vulnerability goes beyond a simple call for "design justice" or "data feminism": it is a call for us to take seriously the messy, ambiguous, and often-complicit starting points that all of us hold in *pursuing* justice and feminism. This means not only designing technology to sit in an otherwise-imperfect world but situating ourselves as otherwise-imperfect designers. It means inverting the cry to "move fast and break things" into a demand that we move carefully, and do so aware of our brokenness.

Notes

1 Agam Shah, "Can You Repair What You Own?," *Mechanical Engineering* 140, no. 9 (2018): 37–41.

2 S. Kyle Montello, "The Right to Repair and the Corporate Stranglehold over the Consume: Profits over People," *Tulane Journal of Technology & Intellectual Property* 22, no. 1 (2020): 165–84.

3 John Law, *Organizing Modernity: Social Ordering and Social Theory* (Hoboken: John Wiley & Sons, 1993).

4 Mark Coeckelbergh, *Human Being@risk: Enhancement, Technology, and the Evaluation of Vulnerability Transformations* (Berlin: Springer, 2013).

5 Erinn Gilson, "Vulnerability, Ignorance, and Oppression," *Hypatia* 26, no. 2 (2011): 308–32.

6 Daniela K. Rosner and Morgan Ames, "Designing for Repair? Infrastructures and Materialities of Breakdown," in *Proceedings of the 17th ACM Conference on Computer Supported Cooperative Work & Social Computing* (Association for Computing Machinery, 2014).

7 Christina Dunbar-Hester, *Hacking Diversity* (Princeton University Press, 2019) and Nathan Ensmenger, "Beards, Sandals and Other Signs of Rugged Individualism," *Osiris* 30, no. 1 (2015): 38–65.

8 See also Os Keyes and Jeanie Austin, "Feeling Fixes: Mess and Emotion in Algorithmic Audits," *Big Data & Society* (2022). doi: 10.1177/2053951722111377.

9 Alexis Shotwell, *Knowing Otherwise: Race, Gender, and Implicit Understanding* (University Park: Penn State Press, 2011).

11

Good Technology Is Slow (to Scale)

Ranjit Singh

We met Ranjit through one of Eleanor's friends, Michelle Spektor, an expert in the history of biometrics. Ranjit explores concepts, keywords, and everyday stories about living with data and AI in and from the Majority World (an alternative to the terms "developing world" or "Third World" that describes the countries where the majority of the world's population resides). This covers everything from experiences of biometric surveillance systems like the Aadhar card system in India to creating resources and primers about AI in and from the Majority World. Ranjit was a joyful presence on the podcast and also brings his trademark creativity, warmth and enthusiasm to his academic work. He introduced to us the idea of biometric systems "seeing" in "low and high resolution," foregrounding some people and aspects of the human experience and obfuscating others. These are not "just" metaphors; we rely on these kinds of ideas to help us understand the true impact of identification systems in shaping our lives and the allocation of state resources.

Slow is a culture. It is a movement. It is a way of life. Slow is a reaction to the increasing pace of life in the fast lane, from fast food to fast scholarship. As Carl Honore,[1] one of the prime proponents of the slow movement, puts it: slow is about taking the time to do something as well as possible, not as fast as possible. Slow is a response to efficiency.

This piece is not in praise of slowness; it is an invitation to it. It connects slowness with scale, particularly in response to the quickness of data systems that have come to shape our everyday lives. It explores scale in relationship to two prominent features of big data systems: volume and velocity. Volume refers to quantity of accumulated data; big volume implies large quantities of data that cannot simply be read by humans. We need machines, specifically computers, to understand it. Velocity marks the speed at which data is accumulated. The greater the velocity, the faster the accumulation, the more difficult it becomes to process data and make sense of it.

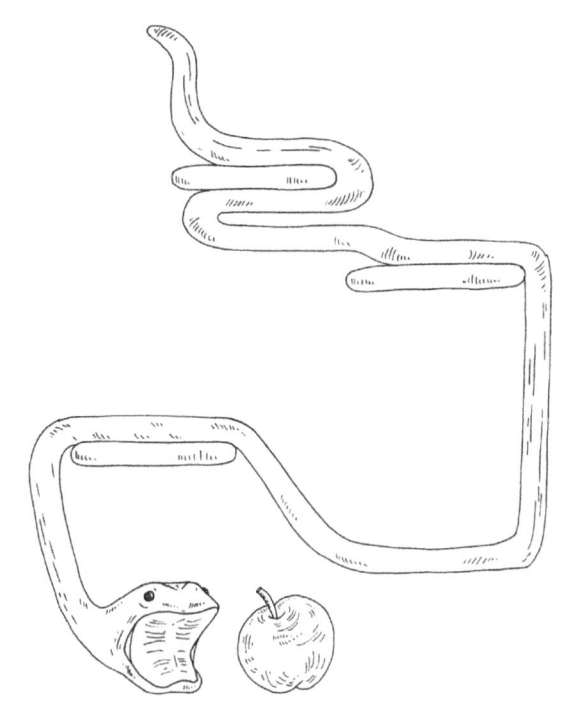

Slowness
This piece is not in praise of slowness; it is an invitation to it.

In exploring a dozen ways to get lost in large-scale datasets, Lawrence Busch[2] begins with a simple distinction of scales in managing the volume of data. Scale in big data operates at two levels: aggregation and individuation. Aggregation involves combining individual data (records or even, datasets) to create large volumes of data. These large volumes of data are processed to find correlations that connect groups with certain characteristic patterns of behavior. Aggregation produces patterns in similarities; scale becomes a matter of managing the largeness of volumes of data. Individuation involves establishing characteristics of an individual user in relation to patterns of aggregated group behavior. The individual only exists as unique in relationship to these aggregates. Individuation produces patterns through differences; scale becomes a matter of managing the smallness of individual datasets.

Scale in managing volume is a matter of establishing relationships between data records. What the data represents collectively is a question of aggregation. How the data represents an individual's place and position in a dataset is a question of individuation.

Scale not only represents but also creates these relationships. In representing the aggregate behavior of people, it creates people who fall into categories of "desirable" behavior. "Trustworthy" people, "punctual" people, "unique" people, this list can go on. These categories of "desirable" behavior inevitably come with their inverse.[3] "Trustworthy" people can only exist in relation to "untrustworthy" people. Otherwise, everyone is trustworthy, and no one is trustworthy. People not only have to fit into these new categories of "desirable" behavior but they also must know when they fall into its inverse and work their way out of it.

Now imagine if this happens quickly. One day you're "trustworthy," the next day you're not. With increasing use of data systems in all aspects of everyday life, these decisions based on sociohistorical datasets and made by machines result in real consequences at a much faster pace. People are left to face these uneven consequences, often without an explanation about how such decisions are made.

Examples of such consequences include the lawsuit in Kenya around the double registration of vulnerable citizens,[4] who have struggled to obtain citizenship documents because their biometrics were recorded in refugee databases. One day you're a citizen; the next day you're a refugee. And the class action lawsuit in Australia against RoboDebt,[5] an automated debt recovery scheme, which wrongly accused about 400,000 welfare recipients of misreporting their income and issued reams of debt notices. One day you're a welfare beneficiary; the next day you're asked to return your welfare payments.

This brings me to the first point that I wish to make with this piece: the pace of such decisions must become slower, especially when there are life chances at stake. This slowness requires erring on the side of generosity and inclusion, rather than efficiency and exclusion.

During my fieldwork on the challenges of appropriating India's biometrics-based identity number in welfare services,[6] a respondent narrated a parable on unanticipated consequences of interventions. It provides a window into this call for erring on the side of generosity.

> There once was a man who pledged that he would feed the pigeons that used to gather on his porch every day. Over time, he realized that there were not only pigeons eating the feed, but also some crows. The moral of this story lies in one simple question: Should this man stop feeding the pigeons because of the crows? And, I believe, the answer should be, "No." (Fieldnotes, 2 July 2015)

Pigeons and Crows
The moral of this story lies in one simple question: Should this man stop feeding the pigeons because of the crows? And, I believe, the answer should be, "No."

Given the inevitability of failures associated with any data system, the work of maintaining "good" data systems must err on the side of generosity.

Erring on the side of generosity involves four crucial steps:

- First is to start small and with multiple pilot projects across places and contexts. These projects must be complemented with existing processes that provide alternative ways to achieve the same goals when data systems fail. These pilot projects offer an opportunity to iterate on experimenting with how well a data system works and its consequences across scales of place and time. These systems can be connected with each other over time to produce data infrastructures.

- Second, ensuring that data systems are incorporated in everyday life linearly (or at a steady rate), rather than exponentially (or at a compound rate). Societal change is slow and tends to unfold linearly, while data systems are fast and grow exponentially. The disconnect between the two often produces breakdowns in how data systems are incorporated in any social process.

- Third, moving at the speed of trust between system operators and people who will eventually become subject to the system for accessing social services. People need time to develop their own understanding and literacy in interacting with these systems. They need opportunities to speak back and seek due process when they face harm.

- Fourth, accepting inefficiencies and errors as a part of the operating cost of the system, rather than passing on this cost on to the people. This happens most often in determining eligibility of a person in receiving a service, especially in the context of targeted welfare services such as RoboDebt.[7] The parable was also in response to concerns around determining eligibility. An automated decision of ineligibility or debt notice (in RoboDebt's case) must not automatically exclude an existing beneficiary from a welfare service without due process.

All these steps take time. They require that we slow down in building and living with data systems.

This brings me to the second point I wish to make with this piece: slowing down has deep implications for managing the velocity of data. This velocity spans from the pace of data collection, processing, and analysis to the quickness of data-driven decision-making. Velocity is often treated as synonymous with efficiency in the discourse of big data.

Its value is often illustrated with a story about selling Halloween cookies at Walmart. This story, as documented by Bernard Marr on real-time insights from Walmart's data cloud in 2017,[8] goes as follows:

> Sales data showed that a particular kind of novelty cookie launched to celebrate Halloween was very popular in most Walmart stores, except two where they were not selling at all. This difference was quickly investigated. The investigation revealed that a simple stocking oversight had resulted in the cookies not being placed on the shelves at all in the two stores. The cookies were immediately put on shelves preventing further loss of sales.

The story represents insights emerging from both aggregation and individuation. While the Halloween cookies were very successful as an *aggregate* pattern in sales data, there were two stores that *individually* were not doing as well as expected in terms of the aggregated pattern. This story is about not just the speed of data analysis and interpretation but also the speed of making real-time decisions based on this data. Had the stocking oversight been noticed after Halloween, the cookies may not have sold at all.

Certain decisions are time-sensitive. They range from simple logistical issues at supermarkets to humanitarian crisis responses. Responding quickly is essential, even if it is with incomplete data. Doing something at pace is better than waiting in hopes of doing it better. However, not every data-driven decision is time-sensitive. Particularly, when it comes to determining life chances, decisions to exclude must not be taken without due process.

Making data-driven judgments on citizenship status in Kenya and welfare eligibility in Australia are examples of such crucial decisions that need time. When decisions are made quickly, they become prone to bias, which often stacks the odds against the systemically marginalized. Slowing down would inevitably involve understanding the unevenness of bias and finding ways to tackle it.

Scale as a matter of managing velocity represents scales of time. This is obvious in every call for due process that demands that time taken to make a decision must correspond with the magnitude of consequences and harms of incorrect decisions for people who must live with that decision. If the potential of harm is greater, the time taken for due process before deciding must be correspondingly longer.

These calls, however, tend to take the infrastructure required for data systems to produce automated decisions as a given. When we open the process of building this infrastructure to scrutiny, we will find that all infrastructural change is slow, whether it is building a new subway line in a city or creating the conditions for the use of data systems in delivering any service. Automated decision-making based on data has tremendous infrastructural momentum. This momentum is a result of the large-scale investment of resources into building data infrastructures and producing volumes of data to inform decision-making. These investments have now become justifications for appropriating data systems in existing practices of providing services. The impetus on velocity comes from these justifications and resulting expectations of quick returns from ongoing investments.

However, existing practices do not simply roll over and change when faced with such infrastructural momentum. They often exhibit infrastructural inertia. Infrastructural inertia does not imply stasis; rather, it is the work required to change existing practices and develop new competencies in transitioning to new processes of data-driven decision-making. Integrating data-driven decision-making into existing infrastructure is slow, because you have to manage the momentum of data systems and the inertia of existing practices.

It is during this slow process of mutual shaping that meaningful interventions in erring on the side of generosity can be made. Rather than reacting to the harms of data-driven decision-making, it is time that we proactively account for its consequences and prepare for them. Whether this accounting happens through algorithmic impact assessments or through algorithmic audits, its effect is to slow the momentum of data-driven decision-making so that its consequences can be assessed/audited before its deployment in the real world.

Let us strengthen the inertia of transitioning to data-driven decision-making. This is not resistance for its own sake; it is the only way of ensuring that the dignity of data subjects is not the cost of efficiency. Being slow does not mean rejecting change. It means embracing change thoughtfully. A technology that enables us to do this . . . that scales slowly and thoughtfully, is "good."

Notes

1. Carl Honore, *In Praise of Slowness: Challenging the Cult of Speed*, Annotated edition (New York: HarperOne, 2005).

2. Lawrence Busch, "Big Data, Big Questions | A Dozen Ways to Get Lost in Translation: Inherent Challenges in Large Scale Data Sets," *International Journal of Communication* 8, no. 1727–44 (June 2014), http://ijoc.org/index.php/ijoc/article/view/2160/1160.

3. Ranjit Singh, "'The Living Dead': Orphaning in Aadhaar-Enabled Distribution of Welfare Pensions in Rajasthan," *Public* 30, no. 60 (2020): 92–104, https://doi.org/10.1386/public_00008_7.

4. Haki na Sheria Initiative, "Biometric Purgatory: How the Double Registration of Vulnerable Kenyan Citizens in the UNHCR Database Left Them at Risk of Statelessness," Citizenship Rights in Africa Initiative, November 17, 2021, https://citizenshiprightsafrica.org/biometric-purgatory-how-the-double-registration-of-vulnerable-kenyan-citizens-in-the-unhcr-database-left-them-at-risk-of-statelessness/.

5. Terry Carney, "Robo-Debt Illegality: The Seven Veils of Failed Guarantees of the Rule of Law?," *Alternative Law Journal* 44, no. 1 (March 1, 2019): 4–10, https://doi.org/10.1177/1037969X18815913.

6. Ranjit Singh and Steven Jackson, "Seeing Like an Infrastructure: Low-Resolution Citizens and the Aadhaar Identification Project," *Proceedings of the ACM on Human-Computer Interaction* 5, no. CSCW2 (October 18, 2021): 315:1–315:26, https://doi.org/10.1145/3476056.

7. Lyndal N. Sleep, "Trauma and Automated Welfare Compliance in Australia," Points | D&S Research Blog, December 14, 2022, https://points.datasociety.net/trauma-and-automated-welfare-compliance-in-australia-ba661a60b50f.

8. Bernard Marr, "Really Big Data at Walmart: Real-Time Insights from Their 40+ Petabyte Data Cloud," *Forbes*, https://www.forbes.com/sites/bernardmarr/2017/01/23/really-big-data-at-walmart-real-time-insights-from-their-40-petabyte-data-cloud/ (accessed November 22, 2022).

12

Good Technology Is Accessible, Not Just "Good Enough"

Meryl Alper

Meryl's work explores how digital technologies shape the lives of disabled children and their families. Her book Giving Voice critically examines the uptake of technologies that claim to 'give voice to the voiceless', examining how voice technologies remain embedded within systems of structural inequality. Her current project asks how autistic children and youth use media and technology, and shows how the social and health inequalities they face spill over into the ways they use technology. Meryl used to work in children's television—including Sesame Street—and brings her extensive experience in children's media and entertainment to her work in communication studies. She is deeply passionate about accessibility, and this shines through in her essay. As a community-focused researcher, one of Meryl's most inspiring features is that she places a great deal of emphasis on acknowledging the incredible work of other disability scholars and activists.

For my book *Giving Voice*,[1] I interviewed a mother of two autistic children, one of whom was non-speaking and used an iPad and a synthetic speech app as an assistive communication device. Offhandedly, I said to the mother that surely one would not want to use the words "magic" or "revolutionary" to describe the iPad. It was a comment grounded in academic training that taught me to be wary of techno-utopianism, and my sociological understanding of how the effective use of technology requires learned techniques that many do not have access to.² She insisted, however, that she did think it magical that the device was enabling what she called "wow moments," or glimpses of insight into her son through his newly communicated perspectives.

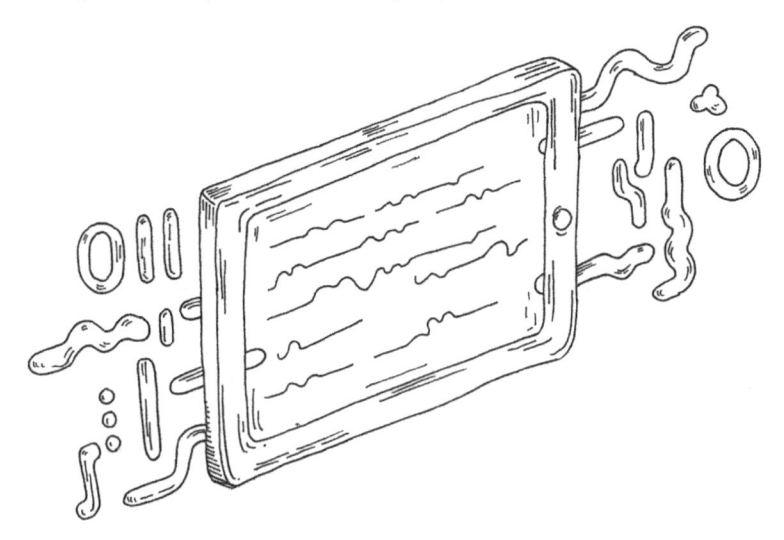

Windows to Communication
Glimpses of insight into her son through his newly communicated perspectives.

This moment of misunderstanding between myself and my research participant illustrates how scholarly ways of thinking about technology are not necessarily more valid than an individual's emotional and affective experiences of them. This is because when we ask philosophical and practical questions about whether a technology is good or bad, we are always talking about more than just technology, but also the society that produced such a question to begin with.³ The most important and vital lines of social inquiry are ones instead that focus on which groups stand to benefit the most or be harmed in the most significant ways by any technology, and how unjust patterns of history (including, but not limited to, racism, xenophobia, misogyny, homophobia and religious intolerance) might be perpetuated or alternatively disrupted through such tools.⁴

This chapter weighs the possibility of "good" technology against the realities of "good enough" through the critical lenses of disability and accessibility. Disabled people are regularly offered up in popular discourse as prime beneficiaries of modern technologies, be it robotics, AI, or ubiquitous computing.[5] Many of these preconceptions are rooted in a deficit model of disability, whereby technology is a means for fixing or repairing the broken disabled body.[6]

To what extent these technologies are "good" is debatable, especially considering the history of eugenic projects prioritizing the rehabilitation of disabled people through technology over their actual physical and mental well-being.[7] It is also worth noting technological developments that exploit disability and disabled people as an "assistive pretext" (a term coined by media historian Mara Mills) for commodification and broader commercial gain, as was the case with d/Deaf individuals and innovations in sound engineering in the late nineteenth and early twentieth centuries.[8] There are wonderful accessible digital tools like synthetic speech that do permit disabled people to participate more fully in society—not just in novel respects but in more powerful ways and on larger scales. But those same technologies, in varied contexts, can also be poorly executed and ultimately end up intensifying and generating new digital and social inequalities.

One example of this paradox of the "good enough" is that of audio captioning technologies. Adding captions to live or recorded video, be it on broadcast television or TikTok, can be useful when audio quality is subpar, while listening in loud environments, or as a stylistic choice.[9] Captioning is culturally packaged as something that can be great for everybody in some form, which is the logic of universal design.[10] But scholars like Greg Downey, Louise Hickman, and Jaipreet Virdi highlight how captioning so often falls short for d/Deaf and hard-of-hearing audiences, especially when captions are not legally mandated, as in the case of user-generated videos posted to the internet.[11]

It is what led disability activist Rikki Poynter to create the #NoMoreCraptions hashtag campaign on Twitter to push back against the notion that AI-powered automatic captioning on digital platforms such as YouTube is a sufficient solution, and that a little bit of substandard captioning is better than nothing at all.[12] Incorrect captions can be confusing and disorienting, which is not enabling, especially when those errors are never corrected. Poor captioning subsequently generates additional labor, be it fixing or creating new transcripts. Importantly, the promotion of "good enough" online captioning as a primarily commercial tool for increasing search capability and improving the precision of targeted advertisements severs the technology from its original purpose, which was deeply political in nature and firmly rooted in Deaf culture.[13] Technology may be "good enough," but good enough for who?

The logic of "good enough" accessibility is hard to dislodge from technological discourse because of its legal, social, and political dimensions, all of which are intertwined and coalesce through ableism. Even though there are US laws that pertain to accessible technology, such as the Americans with Disabilities Act, they are inconsistently and insufficiently enforced.[14] Worse, legal challenges often need to be made to ensure enforcement. This is not just a problem for the disability community, but all social movements. The broader pernicious idea that civil rights struggles ended in the twentieth century reflects a complacency that exists across all levels of society that center a white, male, Western, Christian, heteronormative, cisgender, and non-disabled version of how history has unfolded.

Disability rights violations enabled by technology persist today, for instance, through how health and human services are delivered within the United States. Consider the increasing entwinement of paid care work and technology through mobile electronic visit verification (EVV) apps. Deployed in the name of making home care safer and better regulated for disabled and elderly people, the technology serves to justify the surveillance of home care workers, who are disproportionately immigrants and women of color, as well as violate the privacy of service recipients.[15] The case of EVV apps begs the question of at what point "good enough" technology becomes "bad enough" for something to be done to rectify its harms on an institutional scale?

Feminist perspectives on disability allow us to see how good technology is accessible, but accessibility is more than just technological.[16] Critical disability and design scholar Aimi Hamraie contends that access is not something that we should take for granted, but is rather a point of provocation and conversation.[17] Hamraie calls this "critical access studies." Media scholar Elizabeth Ellcessor similarly uses feminist scholarship to think about access not as something static that has already been achieved but related to how the accessing of media is a constant endeavor, given platform updates, hardware breakages, and corporate mergers.[18]

Shifting
Access is not as something static that has already been achieved, but related to how the accessing of media is a constant endeavor.

When access concerns disability-specific communication technologies (e.g., hearing aids, Bluetooth-enabled Braille readers), it tends to be deprioritized relative to more "mainstream" tools. Such investments in human capital speak to the work of another feminist scholar in disability studies, Tanya Titchkosky, who reframes disability as access to the human experience.[19] Titchkosky asks, how are we valuing disabled people and disability, and considering access as more than just a synonym for justice?

Media accessibility is not frictionless; it involves ongoing and active negotiation among those with different types of access needs, some of which can be in conflict (e.g., those with cognitive disabilities who benefit from "plain language" versions of published material; those with ADHD whose preferred writing styles may be more stream of consciousness).[20] Critical media access studies, as I have written about elsewhere, is about interrogating how disability, media, and technology intersect with other ways that people are marginalized within society, such as race or ethnicity, class, gender, and sexuality.[21] By media access, I refer not only to access to media content but also to mediated access, or how people access human communication through media (e.g., texting, video chat). Thinking about media access in a holistic manner requires consideration of what other barriers besides the purely technological exist for disabled people and their support networks, as well as how society itself is disabling.

For instance, ethnographic fieldwork for my next book project, *Kids Across the Spectrums: Growing Up Autistic in the Digital Age*, took place in Los Angeles and Boston, two cities with immense income inequality and legacies of housing segregation.[22] One Black mother of an autistic son in Boston with whom I spoke received public benefits, including an electronic benefits transfer (EBT) card to purchase food and household necessities.[23] The EBT card also allowed for discounts at local cultural spaces like museums, which are highly mediated through uses of print, audio, video, and interactive media. She noted that though there were special sessions for disabled children at the local children's museum with accommodations (e.g., smaller, less noisy crowds), she did not prefer to take her autistic son to those events. This was in part because the price for tickets was more expensive than if she went on a regular day and used her EBT card. These forms of cultural access were more accessible to her than the disability-oriented day because she was also trying her best within additional social and economic constraints. Her story illustrates how there cannot be one single working definition of media access because disability contains multitudes, nor is there a pure, perfect version of accessibility that exists somewhere because it is always in progress.

While "good enough" technology treats accessibility in a black-and-white manner, good technology—if such a thing exists—pays keen attention to an expanding spectrum of gray shades. Good technology would recognize the important work of feminist disability scholars and disabled academics, especially those like Cynthia Bennett and Ashley Shew, whose scholarship addresses the role of media and technology in the social construction of disability and social stigmatization of disabled people at the intersections of race, ethnicity, class, gender, and sexuality.[24] Accessibility involves labor; in particular, traditionally feminized labor that is largely devalued in society. While looking forward, good technology should also honor how disabled people have historically been technological innovators and those who know "good" best when it comes to their needs and priorities.[25] It is important for the next generation of technologists to see people with disabilities, including those among their professional ranks, not just as the recipients of technology but to learn about them as participants in design, development, and productive agitation of the status quo.[26] Lastly, good technology would recognize ever-present dynamics of structure and agency, and that despite systemic oppression and subjugation, disabled people make active choices for joy and pleasure through and around media and technology.

Notes

1 Meryl Alper, *Giving Voice: Mobile Communication, Disability, and Inequality* (Cambridge, MA: MIT Press, 2017).

2 Jonathan Sterne, "Bourdieu, Technique, and Technology," *Cultural Studies* 17, no. 3/4 (2003): 367–89.

3 Leah Lievrouw and Sonia Livingstone, "Introduction," in *Handbook of New Media: Social Shaping and Social Consequences*, ed. Leah Lievrouw and Sonia Livingstone (Thousand Oaks: Sage, 2006), 1–14.

4 Sasha Costanza-Chock, *Design Justice: Community-Led Practices to Build the Worlds We Need* (Cambridge, MA: MIT Press, 2020).

5 Elizabeth Ellcessor, *Restricted Access: Media, Disability, and the Politics of Participation* (New York: New York University Press, 2016); Katie Ellis and Mike Kent, *Disability and New Media* (London: Routledge, 2011); Gerard Goggin and Christopher Newell, *Digital Disability: The Social Construction of Disability in New Media* (Lanham: Rowman & Littlefield, 2003); Jennifer Mankoff, Gillian R. Hayes, and Devva Kasnitz, "Disability Studies as a Source of Critical Inquiry for the Field of Assistive Technology," in *Proceedings of the 12th International ACM SIGACCESS Conference on Computers and Accessibility* (New York: ACM, 2010), 3–10; Ingunn Moser, "Disability and the Promises of Technology: Technology, Subjectivity and Embodiment within an Order of the Normal," *Information, Communication & Society* 9, no. 3 (2006): 373–95.

6 Rosemarie Garland-Thomson, *Extraordinary Bodies: Figuring Physical Disability in American Culture and Literature* (New York: Columbia University Press, 1997).

7 Jaipreet Virdi, *Hearing Happiness: Deafness Cures in History* (Chicago, IL: University of Chicago Press, 2020).

8   Mara Mills, "Deaf Jam: From Inscription to Reproduction to Information," *Social Text* 28, no. 1 (2010): 35–58.

9   Sean Zdenek, *Reading Sounds: Closed-Captioned Media and Popular Culture* (Chicago, IL: University of Chicago Press, 2015).

10 Elizabeth Ellcessor, "Captions On, Off, on TV, Online: Accessibility and Search Engine Optimization in Online Closed Captioning," *Television & New Media* 13, no. 4 (2012): 329–52.

11 Gregory J. Downey, *Closed Captioning: Subtitling, Stenography, and the Digital Convergence of Text with Television* (Baltimore, MD: Johns Hopkins Press, 2008); Louise Hickman, "Transcription Work and the Practices of Crip Technoscience," *Catalyst: Feminism, Theory, Technoscience* 5, no. 1 (2019): 1–10; Jaipreet Virdi, "Black Bars, White Text," *Literature and Medicine* 39, no. 1 (2021): 29–33.

12 Virdi, "Black Bars, White Text."

13 Downey, *Closed Captioning*.

14 Victoria S. Ekstrand, "Democratic Governance, Self-fulfillment and Disability: Web Accessibility under the Americans with Disabilities Act and the First Amendment," *Communication Law and Policy* 22, no. 4 (2017): 427–57.

15 Serena Oduro, Brittany Smith, and Alexandra Mateescu, *Electronic Visit Verification: A Guide to Intersecting Harms and Policy Consequences* (New York: Data & Society, 2021).

16 Rosemarie Garland-Thomson, "Feminist Disability Studies," *Signs: Journal of Women in Culture and Society* 30, no. 2 (2005): 1557–87; Alison Kafer, *Feminist, Queer, Crip* (Bloomington: Indiana University Press, 2013).

17 Aimi Hamraie, *Building Access: Universal Design and the Politics of Disability* (Minneapolis: University of Minnesota Press, 2017).

18 Elizabeth Ellcessor, "Access," in *Keywords for Media Studies*, ed. Laurie Ouelette and Jonathan Gray (New York: New York University Press, 2017), 7–8.

19 Tanya Titchkosky, *The Question of Access: Disability, Space, Meaning* (Toronto: University of Toronto Press, 2011).

20 Andrew Pulrang, "Plain Language Writing—An Essential Part of Accessibility," *Forbes*, October 22, 2020, https://www.forbes.com/sites/andrewpulrang/2020/10/22/plain-language-writing---an-essential-part-of-accessibility.

21 Meryl Alper, "Critical Media Access Studies: Deconstructing Power, Visibility, and Marginality in Mediated Space," *International Journal of Communication* 15 (2021): 840–61.

22 Meryl Alper, *Kids Across the Spectrums: Growing Up Autistic in the Digital Age* (Cambridge, MA: MIT Press, 2023).

23 Alper, "Critical Media Access Studies."

24 Cynthia L. Bennett and Daniela K. Rosner, "The Promise of Empathy: Design, Disability, and Knowing the 'Other,'" in *Proceedings of the 2019 CHI Conference on Human Factors in Computing Systems* (New York: ACM, 2019), 1–13; Ashley Shew, *Against Technoableism: Rethinking Who Needs Improvement* (New York: W.W. Norton, 2023).

25 Aimi Hamraie and Kelly Fritsch, "Crip Technoscience Manifesto," *Catalyst: Feminist, Theory, Technoscience* 5, no. 1 (2019): 1–33; Liz Jackson, "We Are the Original Lifehackers," *New York Times*, May 30, 2018, https://www.nytimes.com/2018/05/30/opinion/disability-design-lifehacks.html; Bess Williamson, *Accessible America* (New York: New York University Press, 2019).

26 Bennett and Rosner, "The Promise of Empathy."

13

Good Technology Needs an Emergency Exit Door

Priya Goswami

We were put in touch with Priya by a mutual friend, Reetika Revathy Subramanian, a journalist, scholar, artist, podcast host, and activist, and one of the most talented and generous people Kerry knows. When we met Priya, we realized she was just as talented and generous with her time. She was one of the first guests we had on The Good Robot podcast, opening our eyes to the possibilities of feminist ideas in app design. We are often quite negative toward tech development, but Priya showed us that it can be done ethically and serve feminist ends through the app that she cofounded, Mumkin. Mumkin builds on Priya's previous experience as an activist against female genital cutting (FGC); you can find her documentary about the practice, called A Pinch of Skin, online. She then cocreated Mumkin to allow people to practice having difficult conversations about FGC and other forms of gender-based violence. We're humbled and inspired by Priya's creativity and her commitment to transforming the world around her, one conversation at a time.

I felt a wave of panic sweep me as I read about the "Sulli Deals," an open-source app created on Github to virtually auction Muslim women in India. The news first surfaced in July 2021. Women were virtually auctioned for as little as five or ten Indian rupees[1] (0.06–0.13 USD). The images of the virtual auction were later released on Twitter under the label "For sale, #SulliDeals." The web app had names and photographs of a few short of a hundred women before Github (an internationally recognized platform for hosting software) took it down in July 2021.

Six months later, "Sulli Deals" surfaced again on the 1st of January 2022, refashioned as "Bulli Bai Deals." "Sulli Bai" or "Bulli Bai" is a derogatory name for Muslim women. With a name and an image to match, young and bigoted tech creators once again made a public and open-source platform (open to contributions by the public) to humiliate and objectify the Muslim women of India today. I step into the question of what good technology is with this dystopian yet true example.

The question of good technology cannot be imagined without knowing and imagining how technologies can be potentially misused and how it affects minorities and those who are particularly vulnerable in real life (IRL). The disturbing example of "Sulli/Bulli Deals" serves as a reminder that although women weren't physically sold, just with two simple pieces of information, a profile picture online, and a name—bigoted tech creators could make a powerful platform to threaten and dehumanize the existence of the Muslim women named in the app in real life.

The disappointment toward the rising anti-Muslim bigotry in India is a personal one. From 2019–20 I created and launched a chatbot-based app, Mumkin, to enable simulated in-app mock conversations, especially for those who have undergone female genital cutting or mutilation (FGC/M). The chatbot is based on a decade of advocacy work with survivors.

How to open up to your family about the trauma of undergoing the practice of FGC/M? We tried to address this prime question through our version of feminist technology, which is empathetic and safe to the best of our knowledge and abilities. Reading about the "Sulli and Bulli deals" made me wonder how women, particularly the Muslim women we hope to serve with Mumkin, can trust technology if there are so many examples of how technology has let down millions of people, especially cultural minorities all over the world. It also leads me to question how our digital reality, our data, information, and pictures are so utterly exposed and vulnerable when in the wrong hands, and are only as safe as the tech creators designed the technology to be.

So how can we separate ourselves from our digital presence? Today, languages around the globe are rapidly expanding to support hundreds (if not thousands) of well-defined and accepted phrases that separate a person's online presence from the real one. There are many examples of commonly used words for an online self that do not necessarily have a "real world" equivalent. Avatars (commonly used in the context of gaming, VR/AR), profiles (commonly used in the context of social media platforms, etc.), and the Metaverse (prophetically coined ahead of its actual advent by science fiction writer Neal Stephenson[2]) are a few common examples. However, as we grow to understand and adapt to the two selves, the "real" and the "online" in abstractions, such watertight divisions do not hold in reality.

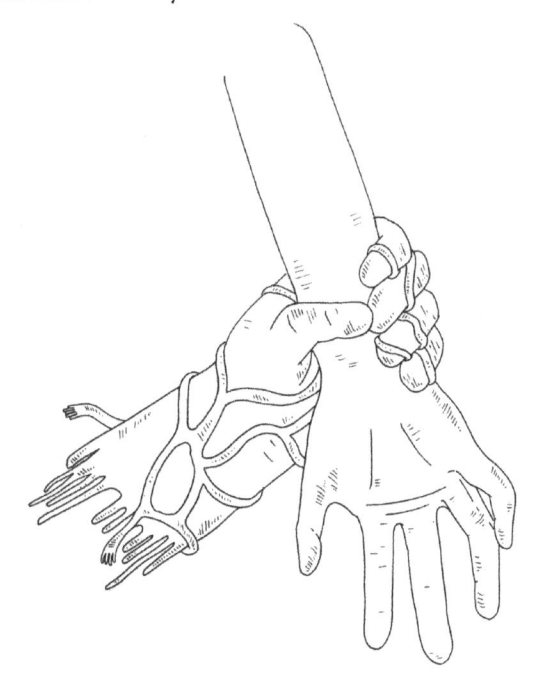

Digital Grasp
As we grow to understand and adapt to the two selves, the "real" and the "online" in abstractions, such watertight divisions do not hold in reality.

Feminist organizations working at the intersection of gender and data justice have often written about the embodiment of data, how online and offline personas merge to amplify biases, and how gender-based harassment certainly extends online. If at all, the question of the segregation of our "two selves"—online and offline—points to the web of the 1990s, which afforded anonymity and a chance for coexistence, especially for the marginalized, such as queer, trans, nonbinary, and disabled people.

As the feminist and executive director of *Coding Rights*, Joana Varon, writes about the web of the 1990s:

> When the Internet finally arrived, it was like magic—here was a positive feeling of autonomy and horizontality emerging, in which we were transforming from media consumers to media creators, finally able to queer genders and let our imagination fly loose with those new tools. Sounded like tools of revolution.[3]

Three decades later, however, it is safe to conclude that the revolution is over. We have emerged from it as walking embodiments of all our digital footprints. Now we are easily traceable, monitored, and even manipulated for gains, as exemplified by the infamous example of Cambridge Analytica. This British political firm infamously used users' data from Facebook to sway people in favor of the Republican Party during the US elections in 2016. It is also probably not a coincidence that Facebook started as the Facemash platform, which rated women. This is eerily similar to more disturbing examples of the "Sulli deals" and "Bulli Bai deals," where women were virtually auctioned off while their appearance was rated in lewd innuendos.

Unfortunately, today, cases of control, manipulation, and subjugation using data can be found a dime a dozen, rampant in any part of the world—be it Iran's latest use of facial recognition to identify women without a Hijab or Google Adsense censoring searches for abortions in America and other parts of the world. These are just some examples of how the subjugation of women's bodies IRL has directly impacted the online information flow and vice-versa.

By investigating the example of the rise of "the Sulli Deals" alone, it is glaringly obvious how the real-world Islamophobia rampant in India today intersects with technology. In an article, the founder of the digital advocacy platform Internet Freedom Foundation of India (IFF), Apar Gupta, pointed out that Github has well-developed policies when dealing with requests from law enforcement agencies seeking user information. This policy could have easily helped to find the culprits behind "Sulli Deals" when it was first launched in July 2021. Gupta then asked why local investigation officers didn't act on Github's policy of seeking user information, knowing that the law had been broken.[4]

Gupta's question about why no swift action had been taken despite Github's policy rings loudly. Unfortunately, whether we are talking about the "Sulli" and "Bulli Bai Deals," Iran's use of facial recognition to subjugate women,[5] or even the monitoring and altering of internet searches,[6] these are all just a few of the many examples of how damning it is when our digital footprints are in the wrong hands.

Given how we are progressing so far, we are already hearing (and ignoring) the clarion call for a plug to pull in case we need an exit plan from the technologies that already govern us. This may not be anything to do with the rise of an evil AI but simply with how today's machines are no different than the exploitative masters who built them.

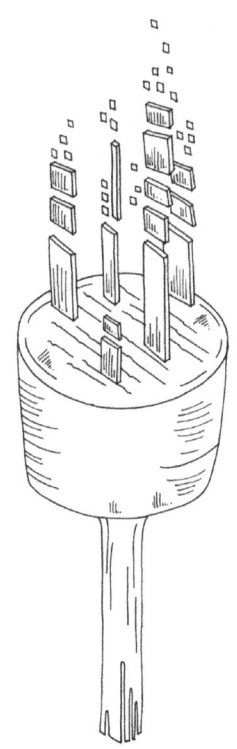

Exit Door
We are already hearing (and ignoring) the clarion call for a plug to pull in case we need an exit plan from the technologies that already govern us.

In other words, growth at any cost remains the overarching motto, as witnessed by the last 300 years of the Industrial Revolution and its technological and climatic impacts. Hence, before inviting any shiny visions of the future, I want to draw your attention to an emergency exit door as understood in the context of the airplane. As passengers, we know there are exit doors as well as life vests underneath every plane seat. This is standard across the globe.

I cannot help but imagine a world with a similar code of conduct, where there is an onboarding experience for each technological platform that we sign up to. I also wonder about the exit doors for our existing technologies. What if something terrible were to happen? Who protects us? And how much time do we have before our digital footprints can be eternally damning?

My vision of a promising technology thus starts with an image of an inbuilt emergency exit door first. I am also curious to see how our current technologies could adapt to better practices, with the most vulnerable among us in mind.

Many big-tech (Facebook, Google, Amazon) companies talk about connecting and bringing people together. But is it really possible to unite disparate people who are not only separated by geographical and cultural boundaries but also by ideology and politics? In a world where political ideology is screened, algorithmically controlled, and surveilled on social media platforms, what chance do we have to create a community with technology?

I faced this problem acutely while designing Mumkin. "I don't know how comfortable I am opening up about my trauma with a bot" was something I often heard while designing and talking about Mumkin. The Mumkin app beta offers simulated in-app mock conversations to open up on the practice of female genital cutting or mutilation (FGC/M), written from a survivor's point of view. Female anatomy is already such a taboo subject across cultures worldwide, even without complicating it by adding a layer of technology. This led us to our central question: How could anyone trust our app?

The answer lies in transparency, even if it means highlighting imperfections. For example, while designing the Mumkin app beta, we could not create an anonymous login page. This was a moot point that we, the team of developers and designers, debated to the very end.

On the one hand, the app would majorly benefit from a one-step login, making it easier for anyone to access it without having to sign up; on the other hand, we had to think about intimate partner surveillance, especially in the context of a woman wanting privacy in a traditional setting where the husband and family members have access to her phone.

It is a tough call, but I am willing to make this trade-off as long as I can be transparent about where and how the data is being used. We don't let any third-party access data belonging to our Mumkin community members. The login system may be tedious, but it ensures transparency and upholds our simple rule—Mumkin is and always will be privacy-first.

At this point, I am compelled to share that I am new to creating technology and do not come from a conventional tech background. Yet, despite our limited knowledge, at a small scale, we could create a system that respects the privacy of any and everyone logging into Mumkin. In that case, why is it so hard for Silicon Valley not to follow suit?

Why do the tech giants not clarify that the platform is free because you, the user, are the product being sold? Even today, mental health apps, health apps, period trackers, and women's fertility apps are hotbeds of data mining, with these apps readily selling critical data to Big Pharma. Some of these apps are free, and some have a "freemium model" (where some of the basic stuff is free, but you only pay if you want to access the lion's share of the content). However, there needs to be clarification about whether or not we have control over our data. This brings me back to my original question of where the exit door is for our online selves (data and more) and how we can get back to a state of self-determination, where an individual has some control over how their data is being used and shared.

I want to default back to the relatively safe web of the 1990s, which, in the words of Joana Varon, "sounded like tools of revolution." I am not approaching this with nostalgia but with the heightened awareness of a new tech creator who began her tryst with technology in her thirties and now is acutely aware of how many times we as users have been shortchanged, misguided, and lied to by big-tech companies.

While mulling over good technology, I leave you with this anecdote. One evening while we were in the thick of creating the Mumkin app, I was asked by the developer team if they wanted me to track the location of our users. "Track location? As in knowing where my users are at the moment?" "Yes," they said. I was horrified. I said no.

Since, I continue to ask myself the question, if a micro-scale app could have chosen to have that kind of insight into an individual's movements, then what power does Big Tech have over us? The answer takes us down a rabbit hole, and I am still discovering where it leads. All I know is that I eagerly seek an emergency exit door in the tumbledown spaces of technology.

Notes

1. Geeta Pandey, "Sulli Deals: Indian Muslim Women Up for Sale on an App," *BBC*, July 10, 2021, https://www.bbc.com/news/world-asia-india-57764271.

2. Neal Stephenson, *Snow Crash* (London: Del Rey, 1992).

3. Joana Varon, "The Future Is Transfeminist from Imagination to Action," *Deeepdives*, July 3, 2022, https://deepdives.in/the-future-is-transfeminist-from-imagination-to-action.

4. Aamir Khan, "Bulli and Sulli Deals: How Can They Be Curbed?," *Bar and Bench*, January 4, 2022, https://www.barandbench.com/columns/bulli-deals-perpetrators-crimes-emboldened-lack-of-prompt-action.

5. Weronica Strzyżyńska, "The Iranian Authorities Plan to Use Facial Recognition to Enforce New Hijab Law," *The Guardian*, September 5, 2022, https://www.theguardian.com/global-development/2022/sep/05/iran-government-facial-recognition-technology-hijab-law-crackdown.

6. "Cersorship by Google Adsense," *Wikipedia*, January 2021, https://en.wikipedia.org/wiki/Censorship_by_Google#United_States.

14

Good Technology Invites Response

hannah holtzclaw and Wendy Hui Kyong Chun

Wendy is an incredible force in the fields of critical digital studies and critical internet studies, and her foundational work was what actually inspired Kerry to start thinking seriously about the relationship between race and technology. Wendy has written widely on topics from machine learning and eugenics through to Orientalism and the internet. She did her undergraduate degree in engineering and now works in the Humanities, allowing her to move fluently and with ease between disciplines and ideas. Her commitment to collaboration with a range of scholars is evidenced by her cowriting this chapter with the lovely hannah, who works with Wendy at Simon Fraser University's Digital Democracies Institute. hannah's work focuses on decolonial approaches to data studies, which combats ways of creating and using data that perpetuate colonial injustices. One of the most striking manifestations of how hannah's work challenges the status quo is how they use creative writing to supplement traditional forms of academic writing. As hannah writes, "if we are to contend with our colonial shadow, to write new stories, reconfigure our horizon, we must first begin with decolonizing ourselves." Decolonization—of both ourselves and the world around us—runs throughout their and Wendy's chapter, offering us new, expansive ways of imagining what good technology could be.

It is difficult to answer the question "what is good technology?" because many of the crises we face stem from attempts to create good technologies, that is, technologies that will solve political, environmental, and social problems for us. The internet, for example, was to end racial discrimination because it was virtual—a cyberspace, in which bodies did not matter; machine learning programs were to offset racist judges by producing "race-free" scores; Alexa, self-driving cars, and other smart assistants were to ease the massive wealth disparities caused by rampant capitalism through "trickle down" machine servants. As headlines "*would you ditch all this chaos for a country in the cloud?*" and "*when the big one hits Portland cargo bikes will save you*" suggest good technology promises a way to program our way from dystopia to utopia.

This urge to program the future, however, is the problem. The clearest example of this is "eugenics"—the early twentieth-century attempt by scientists such as Sir Francis Galton and Karl Pearson to breed "good" human stock to revive the English race. Galton, founder of eugenics, developed linear regression and correlation because he believed such tools could help engineer the perfect eugenic state,[1] from which the feeble, criminal, and disabled would be eradicated. Karl Pearson, disciple of Galton and father of statistics, thought that intelligence, among many other characteristics, could not be learned, only be bred. Thus, efforts for political, moral, and educational reform policies that sought to alleviate the appalling conditions of the working class—such as eight-hour workdays—were a waste of time, since these traits could not be changed. Correlation—used to track traits across generations—was key to proving this was true. Contemporary statistical models that ground recommender algorithms and deep learning for classification (models that determine how we are co-related, categorized, and connected within networks), draw from methods—linear and logistic regression, correlation, the OCEAN personality system, etc.—developed by eugenicists to program ideal populations.[2]

This history matters, not because everyone who uses these methods becomes a eugenicist but rather because when they work, they do so by making the future coincide with a highly curated past. Machine learning programs are not only trained on selected, discriminatory, and often "dirty" data; they are also verified as true only if they reproduce these data. They are tested on their ability to predict the past—past data hidden during the training phase either from within the same set or from a different set—not the future. Just because something repeats the past—for example, a risk assessment program trained on past policing databases that predicts that Black Americans are more likely to be repeat offenders—doesn't mean it's true. The truth lies within the histories and practices of policing and criminalization. As many critical media and technology scholars such as Virginia Eubanks, Safiya Umoja Noble, Ruha Benjamin, and Cathy O'Neil have shown,[3] AI and machine learning systems trained and tested against past data automate rather than learn from historical conflicts, discrimination, and inequities. They close rather than disrupt the future.

These pattern matching systems, which make learning indistinguishable from repetition, forward an impoverished understanding of learning, history, progress, and the future. They frame culture as a program rather than an evolving, situated process. When verified by past data, the future is thus restricted to the histories of contact embedded within and reproduced through the machine—and its designed cultural associations and habits. The work of Simone Browne, for example, has traced the relationship between current surveillant technological practices and slavery, illustrating how "identification" within current information systems is predicated on a history of the Black body being illuminated, knowable, locatable, and controlled as raw material for extraction. This form of involuntary transparency is also a form of knowledge production that works, she writes, to "[alienate] the subject by producing a truth about the racial body and one's identity (or identities) despite the subject's claims."[4] This notion of identification is not peripheral but core to forms of recognition that undergird recommender systems and surveillance capitalism and is key to the evolution and control of meaning, identity, and embodiment within these spaces. This example illustrates the logic of world-destroying progress that, as Ariella Azoulay has argued, reduces people deemed "primitive" to sources and erases the diverse worlds around us that still persist. Against this, she calls for us to unlearn this logic and instead to live in the space of "potential history"—a world that defies a strict separation of past, present, and future.[5] As William Faulkner famously quipped: the past is never dead—it's not even past.

If this is so, what can we do? How do we move away from a future dominated by dystopian threats and utopian promises of escape? For us to disrupt this dichotomy and address the question of what good technology might be, we need to engage different ways *to* think and engage technology systemically. Specifically, through differently embodied forms of learning.

Neither histories nor habits are abstract: they emerge from and are produced by bodies interacting within social conditions and contexts. Thinking through embodied learning helps us face and stay with the trouble of systemic environments and how they come to frame and mark our relationships, experiences, and perceptions—how they automate, delimit, and shape how we see, feel, connect, and imagine. To begin to imagine a future beyond escape or dystopia—to take seriously the ways with which technologies become complicit conductors of cultural, political, and environmental crisis; to truly imagine and enact a world otherwise—we must start with the fact that truth is about relation not repetition, that learning is about discomfort not optimization. To do this, we need to tune in to the embodied conditions of the landscapes we differentially but collectively inhabit.

Right Here Right Now
Imagine a future beyond escape or dystopia.

For example, collaborative feminist performance pedagogy, like that of Dani D'Emilia and lesbian feminist group Colectiva Chamanas of Chiapas, works to recode connections between relationality, affect, and reason by activating the body as a "knowing entity." Though poetic, reflexive, and ethical inquiry and collaborative performance practice, these artists and activists engage embodied experiences like longing, grief, or fear, to design and implement strategies for moving through differences and tensions of systemic change and cultural transformation.[6] Such experiences help us imagine *and practice* new social relations and forms of coexistence beyond those over coded by habitual cultural programs. They transform our understandings of humanity and in doing so expand our capacities to navigate complexity and conflict.

Rather than doing away with the unruly demands and complex contingencies of history, identity, and difference, embodied learning encourages us to *tune in* so that we might adequately learn from them. It provides us opportunities for grappling with the internalized effects of programmability and the ways it constrains both existing and potential cultural and political relations. To respond differently to these pattern matching machines and their reflections, however distorted, of our social landscapes and actions, perhaps the question is not what is *good* or *bad* technology but what kinds of imagined and embodied relationships—to our environment, ourselves, and each other—does technology amplify or contract? For us, *good* technology evokes different embodied relationships that expose and rework designed cultural associations and habits.

Both relational and historical, habits are deeply important. Habits are a form of "second nature" that reveal how others have affected us. Habits both form and connect. Acquired through time and provoked by environmental and social cues, habits are seemingly forgotten as they move from voluntary to involuntary, from the conscious to the automatic. As they do they penetrate and define a person, a body, a group of bodies, a *culture*. A by-product of repetition, habit is tied to implicit memory and reflects our collective cultural unconscious. Within network relationships and interactions habit is a response pattern, a control mechanism that denies us the ability to create new norms.[7] If we can unpack the effects of these technologies in and on our bodies, habit can be drawn upon to locate how, where, and when the past lives on in our bodies—and better respond to the demands of the present.

If habit is a form of history-making, bodies are archives—repositories of things learned and unlearned that contain traces. As gender, critical race, and cultural studies scholars such as Franz Fanon, Judith Butler, or Sara

Ahmed have shown, the body is a deeply colonized, gendered, politicized, and commodified object that both harbors deeper understandings of the systemic conditions we are embedded—and different possibilities for intervening within them.[8] As key sites of both social control and resistance, bodies are essential to a form of critical thinking *with* and *against* technology. The body is a portal for realizing the porosity between technology and the social: for critically disorienting and destabilizing the designed associations and habits that pervade technology *and* culture.

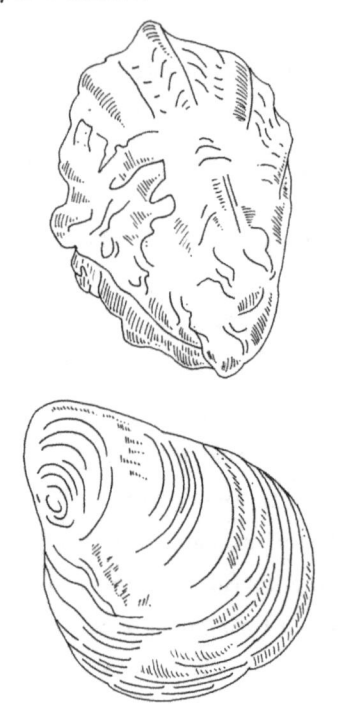

Bodies Are Archives
If habit is a form of history-making, bodies are archives—repositories of things learned and unlearned, they contain traces.

As scholar and performance artist Coco Fusco has argued, embodied learning draws out latent paradoxes of culture and encourages moments of reckoning in personal or public consciousness. It can introduce bodily interactions with technology that push back against the hype of new technologies as catch-all solutions to unresolved cultural problems or "neutral" surrogates for complex social systems like democracy.[9] Perhaps most importantly, it can help cultivate a form of social and technological fluency: it generates both discernment of and creative correspondence with how as we make technology, technology also makes us. In this regard integrating embodied learning into machine learning environments can support us in understanding the ethical dynamics of, and reclaiming agency in, emergent social and technological landscapes and systems.

Within AI mediated social networks—our scripts, our lines are constantly impacted by the actions and words of others—we are constantly, knowingly and unknowingly, marked by and drawn into collaborative relationships with both human and nonhuman others. If correlation works, it's because we are co-related to others. Machine learning through a curriculum that draws on feminist theories of the body and performance would help us foreground the embodied relationships and habits embedded and enacted within our networked interactions. For example, we can critically inhabit and creatively redeploy the network scripts—narrative archetypes, characteristics, value judgments and assumptions that ground classification and analytics methods—of predictive software like the OCEAN model. Through hybrid human-machine performance practice and reflexive, ethical inquiry, we can locate, unravel, and reconfigure the systemic social, environmental, embodied forces that surface connection in these spaces. Such a curriculum shifts the register of how we understand and engage networks—introducing opportunities for re-enacting and reimagining different network politics and futurities.

Good technology fosters sensibilities for understanding the social and historical forces that brought us here and how they move and connect us. *Good* technology refuses to forget how the contemporary fever dreams of enslavement, enhancement, or escape are explicitly entangled with histories of eugenics, social control, supremacy, and segregation. *Good* technology refuses to surrender our collective agency and responsibility within these environments; it refuses to suppress the complex range of relations, the good, the bad, the ugly, that historically ground connection. Good technology enlists and understands discomfort as both generative and essential to social learning—to forming complete and accurate narratives about our shared humanity, to navigating conflict, complexity, and difference.

Opening up rather than foreclosing our understandings of truth, human, and machine, good technology fosters collaborative, creative networked actions that challenge inherited cultural habits and historical legacies; that reckon with and feel into the complexities of interconnection in new (ideally more ethical) ways. Good technology sustains and nourishes engagement with discomfort *and* the distributed imagination—it introduces novel models of togetherness and relationally responsible learning: it beckons forth new forms of social and technological fluency by helping us come to know the world, each other, and ourselves *differently*.

Notes

1 Richard Sumner Cowan, "Francis Galton's Statistical Ideas: The Influence of Eugenics," *Isis* 63, no. 4 (1972): 509–28. https://doi.org/10.1086/351000.

2 Wendy Hui Kyong Chun, *Discriminating Data: Correlation, Neighborhoods, and the New Politics of Recognition* (Cambridge, MA: MIT Press, 2021).

3 Ruha Benjamin, *Race After Technology: Abolitionist tools for the New Jim Code* (Cambridge: Polity, 2019); Virginia Eubanks, *Automating Inequality: How High-Tech Tools Profile, Police, and Punish the Poor* (New York: St. Martin's Publishing Group, 2018); Safiya U. Noble, *Algorithms of Oppression: How Search Engines Reinforce Racism* (New York: New York University Press, 2018); Cathy O'Neil, *Weapons of Math Destruction: How Big Data Increases Inequality and Threatens Democracy* (London: Broadway Books, 2017).

4 Simone Browne, *Dark Matters: On the Surveillance of Blackness* (Durham: Duke University Press, 2015).

5 Ariella Azoulay, *Potential History: Unlearning Imperialism* (London: Verso, 2019), 286.

6 Claudia Rosas Ríos, "The Importance of the Bodies and Emotions in Political Action: A Feminist Performance Workshop in Chiapas," in *Artseverywhere*, trans. Dani d'Emilia, 2019, https://www.artseverywhere.ca/bodies-and-emotions-in-political-action/.

7 Wendy Hui Kyong Chun, *Updating to Remain the Same: Habitual New Media* (Cambridge, MA: MIT Press, 2017).

8 Franz Fanon, *Black Skin, White Masks*, trans. R. Philcox (New York: Grove Press, 1986); Judith Butler, *Gender Trouble: Feminism and the Subversion of Identity* (Milton Park: Routledge, 1990); S. Ahmed, *The Cultural Politics of Emotion*, 1st ed. (Milton Park: Routledge, 2004). See also Lesley A. Sharp, "The Commodification of the Body and Its Parts," *Annual Review of Anthropology* 29 (2009): 287–328.

9 Cuco Fusco, *The Bodies That Were Not Ours: And Other Writings* (Milton Park: Routledge, 2001).

Part IV

Good Visions

Eleanor Drage

For most of my academic career I have sought out feminist visions of the future. I first found these in my undergraduate degree in French and English literature, where I specialized in queer and feminist writing from Hélène Cixous and Monique Wittig to Virginia Woolf and Audre Lorde. I was shocked and mesmerized in equal measure to find Cixous calling for feminist writing in "white ink" (breast milk) and Woolf penning characters that bypassed gender and historical specificity altogether (*Orlando*). Finally, I fell into science fiction (albeit with a feminist twist) in a rogue wine-fuelled final exam essay on Ridley Scott's *Alien* (in which) Chestburster aliens that penetrate male space travelers, and Angela Carter's radical and irreverent collection of anti-fairy tales, *The Bloody Chamber*. The unstable bodies in both texts showed me that traditional ideas about the "human" were in trouble, and perhaps in a good way.

I had never previously been into science fiction, which seemed to me an odd world dominated by men, but these works proved otherwise. If you go to a science fiction convention, you'll find that they are hubs for people who often feel disaffected by the present. Fans are generally lovely and many have given me hugs at the end of meet-ups (this never happens at academic conferences). At conventions in London and Helsinki, I listened to people design different currencies and imagine other worlds and ways of being. I realized that I had been slow to see that the invention of the future was not just happening in tech spaces. Philosophy, literature, cosplay, and conversation were shaping the visions that we have of our "tomorrows."

Of course, society is rather more selective in what it imagines innovation to look like. In mainstream visions of the future, some cultures and technologies are seen as pro-science, cutting edge, and state-of-the-art, while others are not. Many non-Western science fiction writers (some of whom are discussed by Kanta Dihal in her essay) are being sidelined by ideologically rigid fans who take their assumptions about what constitutes "hard science" and use them to police the genre. These entrenched assumptions about what "science" is, which ways of imagining the future are valid, and who has the authority to engage in future-thinking have a tangible impact in tech development. Elon Musk's favorite science fiction books (notably Isaac Asimov's *Foundation Trilogy*) have inspired plenty of new technologies that have little difficulty in securing investment from Asimov fans turned venture capital general partners. Asimov's ideas are being funded by the men who read him as boys, while other wonderful books (by women and people of color) are left by the wayside. More absurdly, if you search the internet for "the origins of AI ethics," you'll see it is often attributed to Asimov's 1942 story "Runaround." With Asimov hailed as both an exemplar of speculative innovation and technology ethics, while Nalo and many other writers are criticized for bringing myth, magic, and spirituality into the future, it is high time we sought alternative visions of technology.

15

Good Technology Is a Portal to Other Worlds

*Felicity Amaya Schaeffer and
Neda Atanasoski*

Kerry first came across Neda's work through the fantastic Surrogate Humanity, where Neda and Kalindi Vora show how histories of racism and xenophobia shape our relationships with robots today. When we reached out to Neda about being on the podcast, we found that she was a great example of why you should always meet your heroes: Neda is unfailingly kind, organized, and an all-round dream to work with. She also introduced us to Felicity's incredible work on border control, surveillance, and how racial fantasies operate across borders. Felicity's scholarship on how the US-Mexico border has historically been militarized, and the current forms this takes through automated border surveillance, speaks directly to two key concerns in AI ethics right now: first, how AI technologies extend previous histories of colonial violence and, second, how AI is increasingly being used to police geographical borders and control cross-border movements. These themes resonate throughout Neda and Felicity's chapter in this volume on how technology facilitates certain kinds of border crossing, and how good technology creates portals to other, better, worlds.

In September 2017, Hurricane Maria devastated the island of Puerto Rico. Nearly 3,000 people died in the aftermath of the storm, which pummeled the island's transportation, communication, and food supply infrastructures.[1] In the wake of the hurricane's fury, Facebook CEO Mark Zuckerberg, along with Facebook colleague Rachel Franklin, donned their Oculus Rift headsets to explore ravaged Puerto Rico. Using "Spaces," Facebook's virtual reality app in which users can create 3D animated avatars, Zuckerberg and Franklin live streamed their virtual tour of the island on the NPR-produced 360 degree footage of Puerto Rico's flooded streets and rubble.

Zuckerberg hoped to make the case that VR technology is a good technology. In an October 2017 Facebook post about the livestream he stated, "One of the most powerful features of VR is empathy. My goal here was to show how VR can raise awareness and help us see what's happening in different parts of the world. I also wanted to share the news of our partnership with the Red Cross to help with [Puerto Rico's] recovery."[2] During the livestream itself, Zuckerberg also boasted about Facebook's role in creating robust internet infrastructures in Puerto Rico. Thus, he found himself surprised that viewers were horrified at what appeared to be voyeuristic disaster tourism—two cartoon avatars slapping each other high fives in the midst of dystopian landscapes of human suffering. At one point in the stream, Zuckerberg's VR avatar exclaims, "One of the things that's really magical about virtual reality, is you can get the feeling that you're really in a place."[3] And, as quickly as VR can teleport you

Mark Zuckerberg (as animated avatar) uses the "magic" of technology to visit Puerto Rico.

into a place, just as quickly, it can teleport you out. "Do you want to teleport somewhere else?" Zuckerberg's avatar asked as a way to end the post-hurricane tour. Franklin suggested, "Yeah, maybe back to California?"[4]

For Zuckerberg and colleagues, the humanitarian possibilities of virtual reality feed into Facebook's investments in building internet infrastructures that support its business model. Raising empathy for the people of Puerto Rico thus serves a double purpose as advertising for the "magic" of virtual reality and claiming that raising awareness leads to recovery after devastation. What is "good" for Puerto Rico is also good for Facebook. This is what new media scholar Lisa Nakamura has called "feeling good about feeling bad."[5] Nakamura asserts that the "idea of VR as an empathy machine that connects people across difference is part and parcel of Big Tech's attempt to rebrand VR as a curative for the digital industries' recently scrutinized contributions to exacerbating class inequality, violating users' privacy, and amplifying far right fascist racism and sexism."[6]

The phenomenon of substituting empathy for meaningful transformation, of feeling bad for distant suffering from the safety of one's home, is not new. This was the topic of Susan Sontag's well-known book, *Regarding the Pain of Others*.[7] What VR offers is the seeming erasure of the distance of the viewer from the space of suffering. Yet, even as VR users can "magically" feel that they are in the midst of a post-hurricane disaster zone and imagine that this simulation allows them to fully know what it is like to be left without food, water and shelter, they can nevertheless return to California as quickly as they arrived. Zuckerberg, as a white male tourist, is free to move in and out of spaces of humanitarian disaster unlike the people of Puerto Rico themselves. Indeed, Zuckerberg's teleportation to Puerto Rico is a fantasy of full access to a place he does not know and from which he does not hail. It is a colonial fantasy of mastery through technology that uses the guise of empathy and humanitarian relief in a way that masks the long history of US colonialism and occupation that have crippled the island's infrastructures, magnifying the effects of the hurricane. VR technology in this context becomes a tool of extending access to Puerto Rico's resources for US capitalism.

Feeling Good about Feeling Bad
What VR offers is the seeming erasure of the distance of the viewer from the space of suffering.

VR proponents like Zuckerberg tout the Metaverse as a more equitable world in which more people can experience travel, opportunities to be consumers, and participation in everyday life. Yet, we might ask, how can we unsettle capitalist versions of "good" VR, like Zuckerberg's, which *simulate and therefore replicate* the same racial-colonial logics of prior US colonial expansions, now extended into the virtual realm? Must a simulation of the world we already inhabit also be a recreation of the same inequities that plague us? Are we rehearsing for a future where hurricanes, floods, fires, climate change, pandemics, excess colonial expansion, and capitalist profit ravish life to such a degree that all we have left are simulations of a beautiful world long ago destroyed? These kinds of simulations take us ever farther from deeper connections with earthly places, people, and ways of life.

A good technology (or a good use of a technology) cannot be one that dooms us to endless patterns of repetitions, in which simulations continually recreate racial capitalist extractive relations (even if the extractive relation is named "empathy"). Instead, *we should think about good technology as a portal to other worlds and other ways of being in the world.* For instance, there is nothing inherently good or bad about the Oculus Rift headset. But how apps teleport us, and how they teach us to relate to other living beings and the world around us, make a big difference.

Elizabeth LaPensée, an award-winning Anishinaabe designer, writer, and artist, created "Along the River of SpaceTime," a VR game that she discusses on her webpage as teaching ways of "relating to land practices, star knowledge, and quantum physics in an interactive non-linear journey about restoring rivers and their ecosystems by activating Anishinaabe constellations."[8] "Along the River of Spacetime" asks settlers to dwell on what it means to be on/in Indigenous land, and to consider the knowledge and commitments to the land as a requisite to entering a place. By slowing down our gaze to see deeply with all life forms along the river, players learn how to repair the complex webs of life in a particular river ecosystem such as the Nkwejong in Michigan. This sprawling virtual riverway enacts Indigenous futurity, a multitemporal place where ancient prophecies and teachings are also the tools to manifest better futures. In fact, according to Susan Bernardin in *Digital Indigenous Studies* (2017), rivers are the oldest technology of virtual travel, an internetworked system that transports people, information, and trade across great distances.[9] To enter into the game is to be transported across scales of stars and waterways, and temporal zones of past-future.

Rather than simply transport gamers from one location to another, the very terms of travel to another place require slowing down through thoughtful perception of the land, a methodology of Anishinaabe scientific knowledge. One must learn about rivers first through knowledge of the stars shining above, before entrance is granted. "Along the River of Spacetime" begins in a wigwam: 360-degree footage allows players to look all around. Players are

Opening location, "Along the River of Spacetime."

then instructed to gaze up toward the opening of the wigwam where one views stars lit up with copper infused artwork. In a 2020 interview, "Artist Talk," LaPensée offered clear instructions: "Look up at stars until they become a constellation." Players can connect stars "through patience, stillness, and focus, [making] constellations of animals appear, unlocking teachings about water, and the role of the stars in activating the growth of medicinal plants."[10] These star constellations are part of the Anishinaabe stories of the riverways running through Nkwejong. Clean water and light from the night sky nurtures medicinal plants such as the nettles growing along the river. By asking players to hone their attention to all life sustained by the river, slowing down becomes a *method of* portaling across spacetime. Players travel up to the stars and down to various locations along the riverways, weaving a story of place through attentive movement.

Unlike the fantasy of access and mastery promoted by Zuckerberg, LaPensée insists that VR teleportation can only ever lead to partial access for settlers. While the game is open to all players, it is geared to Anishinaabe players. LaPensée states, "I didn't want a game that gave away all of the knowledge with pattern memorization and matching mechanics. Instead, I hope for them to be in that place, practicing patience and attentiveness." Any desire for mastery over place fails in a game that asks one to remember—or learn—an Indigenous relation to the stars as the first step to traveling to the beginning location on the river.

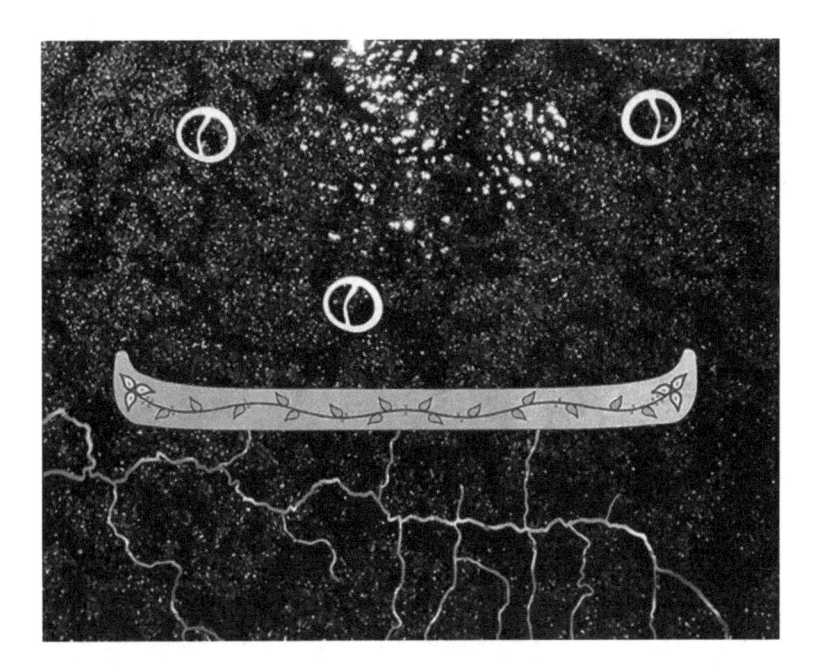

"Look up at stars until they become a constellation."

Players can't simply choose to teleport but they must start by learning to teleport through Anishinaabe teachings and stories. These stories, which are an integral part of Indigenous scientific knowledge, are built into the design of the game. They weave together multiple spatial and temporal realms. Reflecting the journey of life, each opportunity to teleport to another location entails the learning of a skill. "Listen to water teachings. Listen to florals of medicinal plants and foods before you are teleported to the next location in another season in a nonlinear fashion." Depending on the time of year when a constellation appears, you are teleported to footage of a river as it flows in that season. In this way, the land is in constant transformation. Players might learn how climate change heats up the river so it no longer freezes over into ice, a necessary process in the life cycle of self-cleaning. Or, they might follow the roots of trees that purify the waterways. These roots also offer shelter and nutrients to underwater life while the trees' branches reach up to the sky, supporting eagle nests. Or, one might learn how to remove old growth and invasive plants that choke out the stronger-rooted native plants. The game incorporates even more subtle interventions. La

Pensee speaks about singing water songs to the river before filming, which changes how the water flows. Each slight shift causes the entire system to change, a lesson on the responsiveness of an environment to our delicate and careful actions.

Interconnectivity
Players might learn how climate change heats up the river so it no longer freezes over into ice, a necessary process in the life-cycle of self-cleaning. Or, they might follow the roots of trees that purify the waterways.

Even LaPensée's design decisions fortify Indigenous art as an early scientific method attuned to spacetime travel. LaPensée explains, "The leaps in the journey are activated with an Anishinaabe symbol which parallels a particle physicists theorize may relate to teleportation, recently recognized by the LHCb experiment at CERN's Large Hadron Collider." She pairs the massive infrastructure of the Hadron Collider, where scientists "discovered" how to teleport particles across space, with a knowledge practice long held by many Indigenous peoples. One must understand the codes of the game to appreciate these powerful insights. By designing a game where Anishinaabe symbols are the code to portals, players re-enact the power of Native code to teleport knowledge, consciousness, and ancestral teachings across spacetime. Symbol-as-code mashes multiple spacetimes just as it disturbs the difference between technology/art, representation/materiality, primitive/modern, past/future, here/there. As Cheryl L'Hirondelle, Alberta-born mixed-blood Cree interdisciplinary artist argues in the book *Coded Territories* (2014), Native code, or what she calls "ancient semiotics," hold ancestral embodied memories.[11]

Not only does LaPensée's game preserve Native code but the very materials used to design this virtual space—copper and silver to transmit light and energy—are powerful medicines. These metals found in stars and the earth transmit and absorb light and energy from the stars down to the water that reflects back up to the sky. This is about re-feeling the magic of place, which is not the same as the magic of technology.

Training our attention to living relationships takes time. It takes a reorientation of our worldviews rather than frenetic teleporting in and out of spaces we cannot get to know though disaster tourism. Just as there are portals to the same, there are portals to other worlds, other ways of apprehending aliveness, other kinds of relations.

Notes

1 Marisol LeBrón and Yarimar Bonilla, *Aftershocks of Disaster: Puerto Rico Before and After the Storm* (Chicago: Haymarket Books, 2019).

2 Lucas Mantey, "Zuckerberg Apologizes for His Tone-Deaf VR Cartoon Tour of Puerto Rico Devastation," *TechCrunch*, October 10, 2017, https://techcrunch.com/2017/10/10/zuckerberg-apologizes-for-his-tone-deaf-vr-cartoon-tour-of-puerto-rico-devastation/.

3 Arjun Kharpal, "Mark Zuckerberg Apologizes After Critics Slam His 'Magical' Virtual Reality Tour of Puerto Rico Devastation," *CNBC*, October 10, 2017, https://www.cnbc.com/2017/10/10/facebook-ceo-mark-zuckerberg-slammed-for-puerto-rico-vr-video.html.

4 Mantey, "Zuckerberg Apologizes for His Tone-Deaf VR Cartoon Tour of Puerto Rico Devastation."

5 Lisa Nakamura, "Feeling Good About Feeling Bad: virtuous Virtual Reality and the Automation of Racial Empathy," *Journal of Visual Culture* 19 (2020): 47–64, p. 47.

6 Nakamura, "Feeling Good About Feeling Bad," 61.

7 Susan Sontag, *Regarding the Pain of Others* (New York: Farrar, Straus and Giroux, 2003).

8 Elizabeth LaPensée, "Along the River of SpaceTime," elizabethlapensee.itch.io, 2018, https://elizabethlapensee.itch.io/along-the-river-of-spacetime.

9 Susan Bernardin, in her analysis of Heid E. Erdrich's short poem-film "Pre-Occupied," argues "images of rivers and their deltas express the flow, trade, connectivity, and networked structure of the digital and the Internet." See her article, "'There's a River to Consider': Heid E. Erdrich's 'Pre-Occupied,'" *Studies in American Indian Literatures: Special Issue, Digital Indigenous Studies: Gender, Genre, and New Media* 29, no. 1 (Spring 2017): 52.

10 "Artist Talk: Along the River of Spacetime, by Elizabeth LaPensee," *Digital Culture and Education*, June 26, 2020, https://www.digitalcultureandeducation.com/volume-12-2-papers/artist-talk-along-the-river-of-spacetime.

11 "Codetalkers Recounting Signals of Survival," in *Coded Territories: Tracing Indigenous Pathways in New Media Art*, ed. Steven Loft and Kerry Swanson (Calgary: University of Calgary Press, 2014).

16

Good Technology Is/Not Asian Women

Anne Anlin Cheng

Kerry first came across Anne via her work on "Ornamentalism," which Anne describes as a "feminist theory for the yellow woman." Anne uses the term "ornamentalism" to denote how East Asian women have historically been cast as both people and things, specifically Oriental "ornaments." This ornamentalization makes the "yellow woman" "too aestheticized to suffer injury but so aestheticized that she invites injury." For Kerry, it was one of the first times she'd experienced feminist scholarship that spoke so deeply and directly to her own experiences as an New Zealand Asian woman; Anne herself refers to writing this book as a form of therapy. Before Anne's work, Kerry had never encountered such in-depth feminist theorizing on the figure of the "yellow woman," and Anne wrote Ornamentalism in part to respond to the "theoretical black hole" that surrounds Asiatic womanhood in US-based critical theory. Kerry was so nervous to interview Anne for The Good Robot *podcast, but Anne immediately put her and Eleanor at ease. Anne is a brilliant thinker and an exquisite writer, and her beautiful essays in* The Nation *and the* LA Review of Books *partially inspired this book. Anne's work balances sharp critique with poetic reflection, and her scholarship continues to lay the groundwork for Asian American feminists for decades to come.*

What is good technology? I'm less interested in offering a moral judgment and more interested in exploring a set of ethical questions, questions such as: Who or what counts as human and inhuman; what kinds of values are generated when we turn people into things and things into people; what are the unspoken assumptions beneath technological invention, coding, and deployment, especially when they get applied to women and persons of color?

The history of the entanglement between technology and race has been a dysphoric one, and the history of technology and racialized gender has been even more so. Think, for example, of the stubborn association between unfeeling robotics and Asian labor in the nineteenth century to ideas about the tireless "Chinese coolie" or twenty-first-century notions of Asian Americans as efficient but uncreative drones.[1] There has also been for centuries an equally enduring association of the Asiatic woman with excessive, synthetic ornamentality that makes her practically a "thing" herself. That is, "she" is so ornamental as to *be* the ornament itself.

Over the centuries, the aesthetic and erotic work of ornamental Asiatic femininity for Western cultural imagination has turned the Asiatic woman into a preeminent analogy for, or often the very embodiment of, artificial life. This is why the figuration of her as the cyborg gets repeatedly invoked by popular culture, from the highly sexualized and disposable robotic prostitutes running through films from *Blade Runner* to *Ex Machina* to the seductive, murdering geishas in the recent live-action remake of *Ghost in the Shell*. Scholars have come to name this intimate connection—indeed, confusion—between technology and the Asiatic "Techno-Orientalism," referring to the phenomenon of imagining Asia and Asians in hypo- or hyper-technological terms in cultural productions.[2]

If nineteenth-century Orientalism, as famously laid out by Edward Said, refers to a style of thought and a school of knowledge organized along a distinction between the so-called Orient and the Occident, for the primary purpose of allowing the latter to possess and dominate the former, then twentieth- and twenty-first-century Techno-Orientalism offers a way for the West to manage its anxieties and ambitions for industrial dominance, by fantasizing about the East as both technologically advanced and yet intellectually primitive, in dire need of Western consciousness-raising.

Yet, instead of seeing Techno-Orientalism as simply another instance of Victorian Orientalism applied to modern technology, I argue that there is a deeper connection between Asia and "techne," one that we must consider, especially in our current moment of renewed anti-Asian violence. This is a particularly important moment for us to rethink the conflation between human and inhuman, person and thing, provoked by the recurring figure of the Asian robot.

We are all familiar with the history of racialization as a history of people turned into things, with slavery being the most egregious example. Many have already noted the analogy between slave and robotic labor, but there has not been sufficient consideration of the history of racialization as a history of things being made into people: a history of animation, of personification. Looking at the history of racialized gender through *this* lens reveals different ways of understanding what we readily call "objectification" and allows us to see the unpredictable and alternative afterlives of living-as-as-object.

When we say "technology" today, we think hi-tech, but "personhood" (*who or what counts as a person*) is itself a form of technology, a language, and a set of codes. The technology of Western personhood has long been entangled with the language of race and gender since before the Age of Exploration through the Industrial Revolution, which is also to say, since the beginning of Western imperialism and conquests. When we say today that racism and sexism are systemic, what we really mean are two things: first, that these ideologies have a historic precedent; and second, that they have been built, baked, and encoded into social, cultural and technological systems.

In order to address the systemic, we have to go back to how Western imperial colonization has invested in and produced racial and gender distinctions. The history of technology and the history of race and gender are thus so deeply braided with one another that it's impossible to actually think about technology without also thinking about these forms of social categorization: how certain kinds of human bodies have been made to be part of the technology of capitalism and of industrialization.

Braided
The history of technology and the history of race and gender are thus so deeply braided with one another that it's impossible to actually think about technology without also thinking about these forms of social categorization: how certain kinds of human bodies have been made to be part of the technology of capitalism and of industrialization.

In short, bodies are always already implicated in capitalist and imperial economies and their technologies. Technology is more than just a tool: it is the original prosthesis of humanity.

Techno-orientalism as a concept is thus most powerful not when it points out racist stereotypes, but when it affords us a way to rethink the logic of racial embodiment: how race enables ideas of embodiment and disembodiment, how gender enables or disables that embodiment, and how human flesh may be more imbricated with technology than we think. We have this idea that Western personhood is this Lockean, organic, integrated, and masculine subject. But, in fact, the idea of the human has been much more indebted to the inorganic and the synthetic than we think. Even conceptions of legal personhood do not anchor themselves in organic personhood: to wit, abstract entities from corporations to forests can acquire the status of legal person.

Skin
Human flesh may be more imbricated with technology than we think.

There is therefore—and always has been—a mechanical as well as a biological grammar to embodiment itself. The body has always been organic and mechanistic, material and metaphysical. And our corporeal interface with prosthetic things from eye glasses to artificial organs to even our attachments to our cell phones today has always registered our human indebtedness to thingliness. But mostly we like to gloss over or ignore this debt. The myth goes: those "things" exist to enhance us; "we" are never in danger of losing our humanness. With the racial other, however, and with Asiatic femininity in particular, this entanglement with the nonhuman gets celebrated as aesthetics. More than other ways that gender is racialized gender, Asiatic femininity "enjoys" this long and idiosyncratic association with ornamental "thingliness": an attribution of corporeal sensuality based not in real bodies but in real things.

This conflation between the Oriental and the ornamental—what I elsewhere called "ornamentalism"—goes back to antiquity. When Plato spoke of the evils and deceptions of sophistry, he called it "oriental."[3] All through Euro-American letters and philosophy from Plato to J. K. Huysmann to Oscar Wilde to Ezra Pound and Jack London and beyond, you can see this extraordinary characterization of decorative excess as "Oriental" and feminine. You see it too in art history from Impressionism to American Rococo to Art Deco. It's not just that Asiatic femininity is seen as decorative but that Asiatic femininity as a corporeal fantasy can be invoked, sometimes solely, from ornamental thingliness.

The aestheticization of Asiatic womanhood in turn obscures the underlying processes of racialization and denigration. People (including some Asian Americans themselves) have asked what is so terrible about being exoticized. They do not realize or they refuse to accept that desire and denigration can and often do go hand in hand. Nothing dramatizes this heart-breaking insight more than the March 2021 Atlanta spa shooting where a young white man killed eight people, six of them Asian American women, because he was trying to control his own sexual desire for Asian women. The women he killed were mostly working mothers pulling double shifts in a service industry that already put them at risk in a pandemic. The gaping schism between their real lives and the shooter's mental life shows how unreal, how potent, and how deadly the "pretty" fantasy of the exotic Asian woman is.

At the same time, ornamentalism—the conflation between ornamental thingliness and Asiatic femininity—can also point us to a productive reconsideration of some of our most basic assumptions about who counts as a person and who or what a thing. I don't think insisting on "the real woman" is the answer to racist projections, not only because that runs the danger of essentialism (which itself reproduces stereotypes) but also because that refuses to acknowledge how compromised "womanhood" has always been. Feminists like Donna Haraway have long been interested in the figure of the cyborg, not because it is a figure of abject objectification but on the contrary because it embodies the potentials of hybridization and heterogeneity.[4]

So the cyborg has for me been a particularly interesting way to think about the question of the human, the inhuman, the posthuman and how these terms interact with racialized gender. I noted earlier that the robot is itself an extension and expression of the slave logic, which makes the cyborg a particularly layered configuration, especially when you add on the scrim of the cyborg's intimate relationship to Asiatic femininity. Techno-Orientalism is not just a new iteration of Orientalism. It is an opportunity to address and account for a long history of violence around personhood and its relationship to objecthood.

What interests me the most about the cyborg or the android is its indeterminacy, hovering between the human and the inhuman, its unsettling articulation. Technology can be oppressive and objectifying, to be sure, but it can also force us to confront the messy interpenetration of race, machine, and gender. When we parse out *how* technology, race, and gender offer alibis for one another, we arrive at a history of racial and gender formation that in turn redefines how we think about organic personhood.

Let's take as a case study the 2017 live version of the film *Ghost in the Shell*, directed by Ruper Sanders. In this version, Scarlett Johansson plays Major Kusanagi, a cyborg. While the audience knows that she's mostly a machine from the get go, by the end of the movie we find out that there's a little kernel of a human brain and soul inside her: the brain in fact of a young Japanese girl who was separated from her family and from most of her body, killed by the Western industrial complex that came to run Japan in this dystopian fantasy. The girl thus represents the trauma of Western Imperial capitalist presence in Japan.

The big reveal in the plot is that this white-presenting cyborg (Johansson) turned out to be a Japanese girl. Yet, this big reveal actually dramatizes how the Asiatic woman is almost always somehow already a machine in the Western cultural imagination. We might say that the film literalizes the insight that the Asiatic woman is the ghost within the ghost, the haunting kernel in the dream of Western modernity.

The Major-as-Johansson-as-Japanese-girl is at once pretty and a tool, a killing machine, a high-tech female "coolie" if you will. Most of all, she reminds us that it is racialized gender that allows the filmmaker to switch the audience between the pleasure of the Major's inhuman feats and the pleasurable pathos of her condition. Race and gender thus both chart a history of dehumanization and also reveal the agent for re-animating the human in our fantasies of the machine. That is to say, on the one hand, the figure of the Major erases and covers over the racial origins of the Major. On the other hand, it is only when we discover that "she" was really Japanese that we suddenly have empathy for her as a human being. *While the whole movie is about the trauma of whether or not she considers herself to be human, it is clear that the machine requires humanization and sentimentalization through racial identifications.* Race and gender, supposedly repressed by technology, become the very pivots on which we can seek the solace of humanity when the dream of the machine overwhelms us.

It is because the Asiatic woman is always already a figure of hybridity, a conflation of abstraction, matter, and corporeal fantasy, that she can represent both the Good and Bad Robot, at once a sign of futurity and of regression, the Cyborg and the Geisha.

Notes

1. For a history of the myths surrounding the "Chinese coolie," see Eric Hayot's *The Hypothetical Mandarin: Sympathy, Modernity, and Chinese Pain* (New York: Oxford University Press, 2009).
2. David S. Roh, Betsy Huang, and Great Niu, eds., *Techno-Orientalism: Imagining Asia in Speculative Fiction* (New Brunswick: Rutgers University Press, 2015); R. John Williams, *The Buddha in the Machine: Art, Technology, and the Meeting of the East and West* (New Haven: Yale University Press, 2014).
3. Plato, *The Republic*, trans. Alan Bloom (New York: Basic Books, 2016).
4. Donna Haraway, *Simians, Cyborgs, and Women: The Reinvention of Nature* (New York: Routledge, 1991).

17

Good Technology Holds Up a Mirror to Ourselves

Michele Elam

When we stumbled across Michele's faculty page on the Stanford website, we were incredibly excited by her work. Kerry, in particular, was immediately drawn to Michele's scholarship on mixed-race and multiracial identities, and how race is made and configured through AI. We immediately invited her to take part in a number of events and book projects. What we didn't know at the time was that Michele's scholarship would (almost) pale in comparison to her incredibly warm personality. Despite her seniority to us and the incredible career she has already had, she has always treated us like intellectual equals, making time to talk with us, laugh with us, ask for our advice, and discuss the fascinating intersections between art, AI, gender, and race. Michele has also been an advocate of the podcast, sharing it with her students and inviting us to speak to her class at Stanford.

Famously, in the study of gender, you know, gender is considered a technology, a kind of technics, a kind of apparatus, a structural element in how society organizes itself. So if you put together the question about technology in the sense of a device, you know, like a television, with technology in the social sense of the tactical ways that we organize everything . . . it doesn't happen randomly . . . So if you then come to the question, well, "what is a good technology?" what you're saying, if you were going to translate that into a more sociological axiom, you would be saying technologies are moral things. Technologies are things that have value. And technologies are inseparable from how we organize value. —Sarah Franklin, *The Good Robot* podcast[1]

Professor Sarah Franklin, chair of sociology at the University of Cambridge, reminds us that feminisms are not a political "special interest," a narrow angle of vision, an optional (read: lesser) scholarly orientation, a belated consideration. Rather, gender—like race—is both a "technic," as Franklin puts it, and a techne, in the Greek meaning of the word: something made. As the character, Tshembe, in Lorraine Hansberry's play, *Les Blancs*, put it, "Race-racism is a device. No more, no less. It explains nothing at all . . . It is simply a means. An invention to justify the rule of some men over others . . . it also has consequences; once invented it takes on a life, a reality of its own . . . And it is pointless to pretend that it doesn't exist—merely because it is a lie!"[2] And like any technology, the conditions for its inception, design, and deployment—from the gleam in its creator's eyes to its release into the wild—are a function of the social values giving rise to it in the first place.

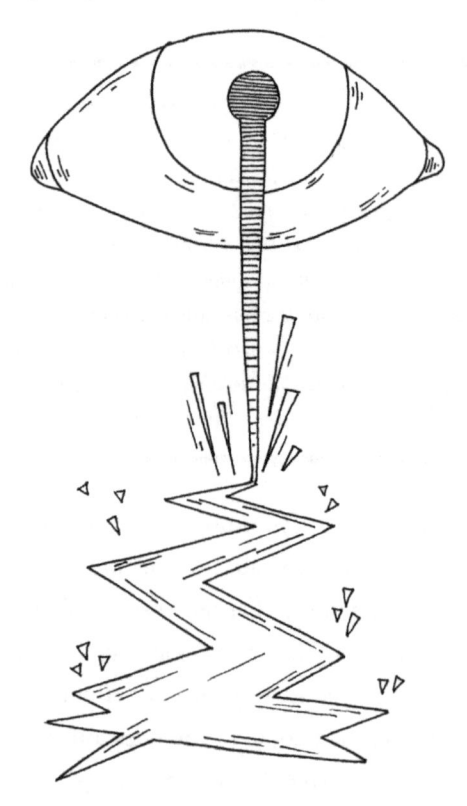

A Device
Race-racism is a device. No more, no less. It explains nothing at all . . . It is simply a means. An invention to justify the rule of some men over others.

To most social scientists and humanists, the fact that code encodes values, that history is encoded in code, may seem self-evident. It may seem obvious to many that tech does not spontaneously appear via divine conception, that it is not a mark of an inexorable teleology of upward progress, that it is not simply individual "genius" but the social environments, economic hierarchies, and cultural Geist that make technologies possible, viable, valuable.

But the mantra of many people in STEM and in the tech industry is still that tech does not embed social values and valuations because it is putatively, inherently, neutral; as the argument goes, tech is only as "good" or "bad" as its users and (mis)applications. This mindset equates to something akin to: Blameless Tech, Bad Actors. (If this sounds nearly identical to the pro-gun lobby argument in the United States, it is no accident—both attitudes share similar assumptions about "the way the world works" about the policies that stem from and maintain that working order). But as many feminists have argued better and long before me, gender and racial binaries continue to structure those worlds, and thus necessarily inform the most foundational aspects of and assumptions about technology as well.

If the linking together of guns, gender, and AI seem an overreach, just consider the opening scene in Stanley Kubrick's 1968 classic, *2001: Space Odyssey*, often considered an ur-narrative of AI. It has a special hold on the imagination of generations who have internalized the assumptions in the opening minutes of that film, in which technological innovation and tribal violence are birthed together—indeed, are represented as necessary for the advance of humankind. Within the first few minutes of the movie, we witness humankind's first tool—a large bone—being used to kill another human. The prelapsarian moment of human harmony earlier portrayed is now lost in the name of knowledge. After the murder, our humanoid ancestor flings the weapon high into the air and the film cuts to its continuing arc into our near future, the bone now a satellite in space.

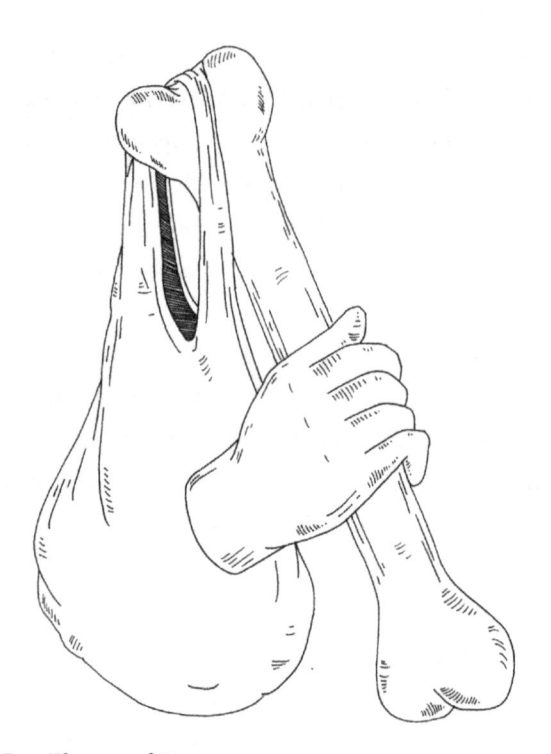

Bone/Carrier Bag Theory of Fiction
Technological innovation and tribal violence are birthed together—indeed, are represented as necessary for the advance of humankind.

The policy implications of that opening are far-reaching: first, it implies that technology will likely always be harmful in one way or another; in other words, legislation and regulation of AI will likely always be ineffective at best and, at worst, impede the "natural" pace of innovation. Society goes from breaking heads in the movie to Zuckerberg's motto "move fast and break things."[3] Second, that human beings are innately violent; we hear that refrain to this day from certain quarters that claim interracial strife is just an "ancient cycle" so reform is futile in the face of our atavism. In short, the film's flawed mis-mash of Social Darwinism and biological determinism is naturalized into just-the-way-the-world-is.

The gendered social norms are also already being midwifed in this tech-birthing scene, in which the actors and agents of violence—and in the film's logic, therefore of generation, change, and innovation—are all figured as male. The passive females cower to the side as the dominant bone-wielding male brains the perceived interloper. The social arrangements are represented as a given, and that given is patriarchal. Film, like all cultural storytelling, is an extremely powerful influence, and in this case bias is baked into the innovation script at the level of semantics. It is therefore unsurprising that the gross disproportion of men to other genders in STEM fields and in AI especially persists as views of what constitutes a technologist, a scientist, a maker in the world are framed through a masculinist lens.

Not accidentally, then, technologists have acquired outsize reach and elevated cultural influence, especially those deemed (or self-anointed) as "geniuses." The fetish for geniuses in the tech world enshrines the Great Man theory: the belief that a few exceptionally gifted, providentially tapped (men) make history, make art, make the world go round—are the Authors and Arbiters of All Things. And this cherished idealization of the singular genius, the sui generis iconoclast, makes it harder to acknowledge let alone credit the people (often women in the tech world), the collaborations, the process, and the collective labor that go into invention. It also means that everyone else ends up living in the imaginations of a very few, as Ruha Benjamin often has put it, who have the leverage to realize their world and worldview. Moreover, the few women currently in AI have been the subject of both racialized and gendered criticism of an often distinctively ad hominem nature, marking them as out of place, unbelonging, and/or otherwise suspect as knowledge-producers.

Such myth-making continues to saturate many of the most taken-for-granted narratives about AI. N. Katherine Hayles notes the overlooked centrality of gender, for instance, in accounts of the Turing Test as the initial basis by which to measure the human-like capabilities of machine learning. As she puts it,

> . . . the part of the Turing test that historically has been foregrounded is the distinction between thinking human and thinking machine. Often forgotten is the first example Turing offered of distinguishing between a man and a woman. If your failure to distinguish correctly between human and machine proves that machines can think, what does it prove if you fail to distinguish woman from man? *Why does gender appear in this primal*

scene of humans meeting their evolutionary successors, intelligent machines? What do gendered bodies have to do with the erasure of embodiment and the subsequent merging of machine and human intelligence in the figure of the cyborg? [emphasis mine].[4] I would argue, then, that the Turing Test—and its ilk—are not really tests of the computer's ability to mimic us; it is a test of *us*, a cultural metric of what and who is considered human.

It seems to me, then, that the processes by which socially transformative tech such as AI indexes "humanity" itself is a somewhat more foundational question than the problem of counting and categorizing human types, which has often and rightly been critiqued. As D'Ignazio and Klein neatly put it: "The ethical complexity of whether to count gender, when to count gender, and how to count gender illuminate the complexity of acts of classification against the backdrop of structural oppression. Because when it comes to data collection, and the categories that structure it, there are power imbalances up and down, side to side, and everywhere in between."[5] The Enlightenment legacy of trying to taxonomize, to name, to capture all things within a paradigm, for purposes because simply the accumulation of knowledge is, at base, an exercise of power. Inequities or "disparate impacts" are too often thought of as merely annoying biases that can be corrected (either by a tech fix or diversity training) rather than institutional undergirding to a social order informed by power relations. That social order is the water in which we swim, the invisible fish tank in which we create things.

Thus the sly wink behind the editors' question of what is "good" or "bad" tech is their reminder that such questions are most often *not* taken as an ethical and moral provocation. Instead the terms gain traction in commercial environments where goodness or badness are collapsed into the vernaculars of optimization, scale, speed, profit, and mitigation of "risk."

In that context, what counts as "good" or "bad" is often taken at face value in industry and academia where human-computer interaction, social robots, and other assistive technologies are being designed and marketed. The long history of gendered and racialized associations with "good"—think of all the damage to people's lives over the centuries by notions of what it means to be a "good girl" or "good servant"—is often lost or misunderstood by even the most well-meaning of technologists. What if by a "good" robot, for instance, we did not take for granted the "good" of developing social robots that did housework or engaged in eldercare. What if we asked instead, what systems of work-life balance are *not* in place that led us to invest in robotics that take over this already-devalued domestic labor, statistically handled by women, and historically, by women of color. And what if assistive "care" meant putting in place opportunities and policies for enhanced social interaction with those in medical need, increased institutional support networks, a rebalancing of gendered work in and outside the home, the re-valuation of care of self and others as worthy and essential labor. What if we invested first and more in those higher-order whole-person solutions than in the robotic retrieval of a dropped utensil or remote monitoring for a potential fall.

We must let the question of what is good tech point not to Turing-like Tests but to ourselves, and to the greater and urgent project of us taking the measure of the social values informing the question itself. Only then can we ask instead: What is "good tech" good for and for whom?

Notes

1 Sarah Franklin, interview with Kerry McInerney and Eleanor Drage, *The Good Robot*, podcast audio, September 20, 2022, https://podcasts.apple.com/ca/podcast/sarah-franklin-on-reproductive-technologies-and/id1570237963?i=1000580049157.

2 Lorraine Hansberry, *Les Blancs* (New York: Random House, 1972), 121.

3 Jim Merithew, "Mark Zuckerberg's Letter to Investors: 'The Hacker Way,'" Wired.com, https://www.wired.com/2012/02/zuck-letter/ (accessed February 1, 2012).

4 N. Katherine Hayles, "Prologue," in *How We Became Posthuman: Virtual Bodies in Cybernetics, Literature, and Informatics* (Chicago: University of Chicago Press, 1999), xii.

5 Catherine D'Ignazio and Lauren F. Klein, *Data Feminism* (Cambridge, MA: MIT Press, 2020), 111.

18

Good Technology Needs Good Stories

Kanta Dihal

Still in her early thirties, Kanta has achieved far more than either of us could ever dream of; she's the editor of multiple books; has published widely in the fields of science communication studies, AI ethics, and race and technology; has received numerous accolades, including the CogX "Rising Star in AI" award and the 100 Brilliant Women in AI Ethics—Hall of Fame; and led influential public facing work like the Better Images of AI project, which provides journalists with alternatives to the white plastic android stock images that populate the internet. Somehow alongside all of this, Kanta also manages to be a deeply thoughtful and caring person, someone who leads by example and is willing to take on some of the more mundane and undesirable parts of group research.

Stories shape science. What is often presented as an objective, truth-seeking, rational enterprise is motivated by dreams and wishes, hopes and fears, and a history of people imagining how their findings might change the future. And if stories shape science, stories create technology. This is particularly true for AI, which is a technology that builds on a 3,000-year history of people telling stories about machines that can think, act, speak, and love like humans. What could be considered the first artificial servants appear in Homer's *Iliad* (*c.* 800 BCE); the first seductive android in Lie Yukou's *Liezi* (*c.* 400 BCE); and the first killer robot in Apollonius Rhodius's *Argonautica* (*c.* 300 BCE).[1] Together, the science and the stories shape the perceptions, expectations, and acceptance of (or resistance to) the many things that are now being called AI.

Being able to hark back to ancient stories can be very helpful. My research has led me to look at both quantum physics and AI, and the difference between talking about a radically new and previously unimagined field of science and one that has its roots in storytelling is vast. AI needs no elaborate introduction: the vast majority of people have some intuitive understanding of what the term means, even if they may struggle to put an exact definition into words when prompted. This is mostly thanks to the many stories that have been told about AI through the ages: nearly everyone can name an example, from Isaac Asimov's robot stories to blockbuster films such as *WALL-E* and *The Terminator*. The term "AI" itself got a major popularity boost in 2001 from Steven Spielberg's film *AI: Artificial Intelligence*.

This intuitive understanding—what philosophers of science call "tacit knowledge"—can be incredibly useful for journalists, writers, and other communicators.[2] AI is a very complex range of technologies, and being able to draw comparisons to things people may have already read about or seen on TV can help with making sense of the incredibly rapid ways in which these technologies have come to affect our everyday lives. But the relationship between fiction and technology is not always positive. As a science communication researcher, I am particularly interested in the point at which the relationship between these stories and technologies creates problems: when there is a mismatch of expectations between stories and reality; when the hopes and fears expressed in stories get misinterpreted; or when stories twist reality in ways that could be harmful. For example, even though it has been nearly forty years since *The Terminator* first came out, it is still the most influential idea of what a lethal autonomous killing machine looks like. This is partly due to media coverage of "killer robots" that uses Terminator images. The problem is that, while these look scary, they also suggest autonomous weapons do not exist yet—but the US air force has been using its autonomous Reaper drones since 2001. And many people in the UK believe that AI and robots are the same thing, and that such robots will (or already do) look a lot like humans,[3] yet the real, existing technology that we call "AI" runs on enormous rows of computers in underground data centers.

However, many other parts of the world see AI very differently: for example, as a tool wielded by a small group of people whose intentions are a threat to our jobs, futures, and even lives. Such conflicts between expectations and reality happen particularly often when marginalized groups come into contact with narratives and technologies that do not relate to us or speak to our concerns and views about the world. Take, for example, exclusions related to gender. People who do not see their identities, bodies, or genders represented in either the stories about the technologies or in the technologies themselves have little reason to think that AI is going to be beneficial. People who see AI itself depicted as looking like the humans who have historically been excluding and marginalizing them would naturally suspect that these technologies put them at risk of further marginalization and harm.

This is a problem that arises with using the stories of our past, which explored the technologies of their sometimes very distant future—a future in which we are living now, but which looks very different to what the stories imagined. At the same time, the majority of the most famous and influential of these stories were written by a very narrow demographic of North American and British white male science fiction writers. This means that there are two gaps between the stories about AI and the reality of the technology: temporal, stories written long before the technology was built, and demographic, stories written by a narrow group of people that do not represent the vast majority of people whose lives are affected by AI.

Despite these gaps, these stories have strongly shaped perceptions and expectations of the technology, what it is, what it looks like, and who it is for. For example, a century of filmmaking has given us over 150 popular films about AI, but my colleagues and I found only eight female AI scientists in this entire body of work.[4] The expectation that someone who builds AI is male is reinforced by over 90 percent of films. Similar expectations and perceptions exist around other historical biases and preconceptions that large parts of society nowadays are trying hard to break out of, relating to characteristics such as ethnicity, sexuality, (dis)ability, and age. Many people are affected by biases around several of these characteristics at once.

If there is one term I want you to take away from this chapter, it is "intersectionality." Coined by Kimberlé Crenshaw in 1989, intersectionality refers to the ways in which different aspects of your identity together shape the privilege and oppression you experience.[5] For example, Black men and women all experience racism; Black and White women all experience sexism; these two characteristics together shape the specific kind of discrimination that Black women experience. As Catherine D'Ignazio and Jen Lee also explore in this book, these kinds of intersections exist across a wide range of characteristics, including disability, gender, sex, ethnicity, class, caste, and race. Intersectionality is a term that should be understood more widely in the world of AI, especially now that the field of AI ethics is really burgeoning and there is a lot of attention on the relationship between AI and gender. Such issues are still often approached in a non-intersectional way, for example, as part of very narrow conversations about "women in AI" or "women in tech."

But across these intersections, people have been imagining alternative ways in which AI could be a force for good, or more accurate ways in which AI might be a force for evil in the near future. Looking across national, linguistic, and cultural borders, we can find narratives that can help break out of the narrow, stereotyped depictions of AI that currently shape far too much of the communication of real developments in AI technology. Narratives that are grounded in different parts of the world, in different systems of thinking, show precisely how the narratives that people in the West are exposed to are also local in their ways: a concept called "situated knowledges."

For example, take the "AI takeover" or "robot apocalypse" story so prevalent in Western science fiction such as *The Terminator* and *Matrix* franchises. It is a narrative that seems to suggest that we humans cannot live peacefully alongside other beings of equal or superior intelligence; that one must necessarily destroy the other. But a range of East Asian philosophies, including Daoism, Buddhism, and Confucianism, have long harbored very different ways of understanding what it means to live with other intelligences, beings, souls, as equal constituent parts of a greater whole. From a perspective that takes humans as the species that should rule Earth because of our superior intelligence, we would be contending for supremacy with a machine that is as intelligent as a human as soon as we manage to create one. But a philosophy that has always imagined humans as one of many different ways of being intelligent, being connected to each other, and being an embodied soul, can easily fit AI into that framework. From this perspective of connection and interdependence it is much easier to imagine coexistence without vying for supremacy.

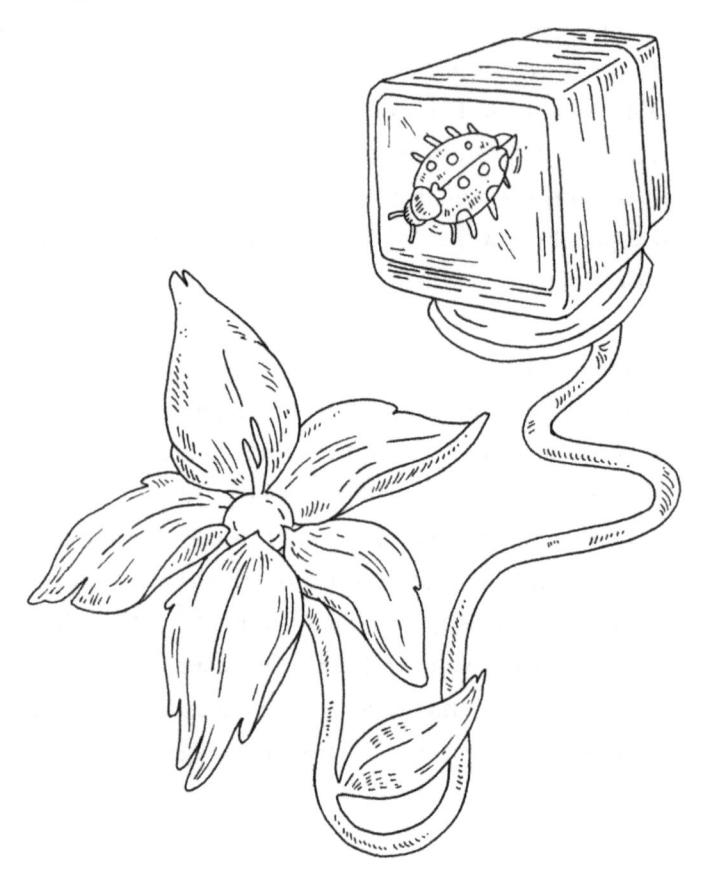

Care Robots
The most popular fiction featuring AI in twentieth-century Japan depicts robots that are friendly and helpful, and only occasionally look like humans.

Japan has distinguished itself as having a particularly positive view of a future with AI. Here, we can see the combination of a history of fictional narratives and current technological developments taking a very different direction. The most popular fiction featuring AI in twentieth-century Japan depicts robots that are friendly and helpful, and only occasionally look like humans. The blue robot cat Doraemon first appeared in a manga in 1969, traveling from the future to take care of a ten-year-old boy. Doraemon has since grown to become a national symbol for Japanese approaches to AI and robotics, being appointed as the nation's first "anime ambassador" in 2008. In a similar vein, the even older *Astro Boy* franchise (1952) revolves around an android boy who becomes a surrogate son and companion in fighting injustice. Stories like these have shaped Japanese attitudes toward AI to be significantly more positive, and much more receptive toward technologies such as care robots.

Intersectionality
A philosophy that has always imagined humans as one of many different ways of being intelligent, being connected to each other, and being an embodied soul, can easily fit artificial intelligence into that framework.

Such alternative perspectives have also been explored in Western countries, in cultures that have been marginalized from the mainstream. Afrofuturism, a movement created by the African diaspora that is particularly strong in the Americas and the UK, and Africanfuturism, its counterpart on the African continent, have responded to AI technologies and their narratives in ways that range from resistance and rejection to reframing and re-appropriation. They are counternarratives that tend to either suggest that these new technologies coming out of the Global North can solve everyone's problems, or that these technologies will create an apocalypse. Neither of these approaches is helpful when the Global North's past technologies have already created an apocalypse for your people. So, instead, novels such as Nalo Hopkinson's *Midnight Robber* and Nnedi Okorafor's *Binti* trilogy imagine what it would be like if, respectively, Caribbean and Himba people were in control of the ways in which advanced technology enters and supports their own cultures and values, rather than having to integrate Silicon Valley technology, and Hollywood perspectives on that technology, into their lives.

Equally fascinating are the narratives that imagine how a future with AI might shape or change our views of gender and sexuality, in ways that give more room and opportunity to people currently marginalized because of their gender identity or sexual orientation. A great example is the robot Paladin in Annalee Newitz's novel *Autonomous* (2017). Designed as an intelligent autonomous weapon, Paladin struggles with its gender identity, first developing a male gender identity and then a more female one. Written by a transgender author, this perspective is a breath of fresh air after the countless stories about men entering sexual relationships with their female-looking robot and ending up hurt because the robot is not what they had dreamed of: a plot found throughout the history of film from *Metropolis* (1927) to *Ex Machina* (2015).

More ethical communication of contemporary AI technology will require us to draw on a broader range of narratives than is currently happening—and as I have tried to show here, those narratives do exist. We can use these stories as alternatives to the endless references to the Terminator or to Asimov's laws of robotics. While this in itself will of course not solve the ethical problems that many contemporary AI technologies unfortunately raise, it can achieve the important goal of making the communication around AI more accurate and targeted toward its intended audience. We need better communication around AI to represent the diversity of ways in which it is going to impact different people around the world—and the diversity of dreams that have explored what that impact is going to look like.

Notes

1 Stephen Cave and Kanta Dihal, "Ancient Dreams of Intelligent Machines: 3,000 Years of Robots," *Nature* 559, no. 7715 (2018): 473–5, https://doi.org/10.1038/d41586-018-05773-y; Yan Wu, "Artificial Intelligence in Chinese Science Fiction: From the Spring and Autumn and Warring States Periods to the Era of Deng Xiaoping," in *Imagining AI: How the World Sees Intelligent Machines*, ed. Stephen Cave and Kanta Dihal, trans. Jack Hargreaves (New York: Oxford University Press, 2023), 361–72.

2 Michael Polanyi, *Personal Knowledge: Towards a Post-Critical Philosophy* (Chicago: University of Chicago Press, 1958).

3 Stephen Cave, Kate Coughlan, and Kanta Dihal, "'Scary Robots': Examining Public Responses to AI," in *Proceedings of the 2019 AAAI/ACM Conference on AI, Ethics, and Society, AIES '19* (New York: ACM, 2019), 331–7, https://doi.org/10.1145/3306618.3314232.

4 Stephen Cave et al., "Who Makes AI? Gender and Portrayals of AI Scientists in Popular Film, 1920-2020," *Public Understanding of Science*, 2023.

5 Kimberlé Crenshaw, "Demarginalizing the Intersection of Race and Sex: A Black Feminist Critique of Antidiscrimination Doctrine, Feminist Theory and Antiracist Politics," *University of Chicago Legal Forum* 1989 (1989): 139–68.

Part V

Good Rebellions

Eleanor Drage

Feminism does not shy away from rebellion. Its insurrections are often divisive and provocative, changing history and overturning the status quo. I will always have the images of recent feminist uprisings etched into my memory: from the tens of thousands of women who marched in Argentina's Ni una menos protests in 2015 to women standing defiantly on cars in the 2022 Iran Protests. These rebellions required women to participate in the double bind of putting themselves at risk for the sake of the freedom of their bodies. Rebellion is a risky business, and for many endangering themselves to change their situation is not a choice. The process of rebellion too can be life-saving for many: a reminder of human dignity, solidarity, friendship, justice, liberation, and beauty. These are the things that I see in both the uprisings that make it onto the news and those that do not.

When we hear "feminist rebellion," we may think first of organized feminist political uprisings. But this book is also concerned with the countless small acts of rebellion in the name of feminism that have gone unaccounted for in the history books. Perhaps you have even engaged in one or two yourself. Documented in this chapter are crucial acts of rebellion that are proving influential in getting generations and populations to rethink their relationship to technology. Jack Halberstam, a hugely influential Professor at Columbia University in New York and one of the stars of queer theory, urges young people to "get off" social media and recognize that they are naive to think these are mere communication platforms. His colleague at Columbia, Frances Negrón-Muntaner, recounts how she repurposed an ATM to offer Puerto Ricans a different kind of currency, one that brought them back to what they value most. These bold and courageous participants are venturing off the beaten track to call for change. Of course, rebellions require courageous voices, and Jack Halberstam, Frances Negron-Mutaner, Catherine D'Ignazio, and Katherine Chandler are four such spokespeople.

While they are all rebellious, I'd like to draw attention to the different rebellious personalities of these chapters. Negron-Mutaner's is joyful, and her joy provides a way to be courageous, perseverant, and humble. D'Ignazio's has the even, personable energy of a seasoned collaborator, a deft hand at justifying feminism's presence in data science spaces. Halberstam has strength and disillusionment in equal measure, seeking not small improvements but a radical overhaul of the system. Kate's piece is both sweeping in scale yet so rich in the small details, showing how change happens in ways both big and small, fast and slow. These chapters offer a range of ways of being rebellious allies and leaders, the kinds that we too can also become.

19

Good Technology Challenges Power

Catherine D'Ignazio

Catherine was one of our first guests on the podcast. We were already big fans of Data Feminism, *a beautiful book coauthored with Lauren Klein about how feminist principles could transform data science. We were impressed by the clarity and persuasiveness of the book and its appeal to people with both STEM and humanities backgrounds. It felt truly feminist both in the ideas that they were pitching and in their collaboration with each other, their referencing of other projects, and their pairing with particular communities to do data work. Being a feminist isn't just about the content of your books, and you can tell what professors are like on the basis of how they treat junior academics. Catherine was extremely generous in her enthusiasm for our nascent podcast and our careers as academics. Trained as an artist, designer, and software developer, she applies her multidisciplinary interests to civic engagement, whether that be reproductive justice hackathons, data visualizations that envision the future of sea level rise, or projects that improve data literacy.*

Lauren Klein and I often get asked the question of what is important about outlining a feminist approach to data science versus just "good" data science. I always respond by saying that the feminist project centers on power. That's why the first two chapters of our book are "Examine Power" and "Challenge Power." For technology to be "good" it must challenge power. This is to say that it must participate in rectifying the structural inequalities that exist all around us in the world. Our world is deeply unequal and this affects the production of data: inequality, injustice, bias, and discrimination all show up in data, just as they show up in our institutions. Data are not born; they are made. They come from somewhere and they are shaped by the conditions in which they emerge. And yet, data can still also be applied to feminist, justice-oriented, and anti-racist applications.

How exactly? The first question around good is, whose good? Good for whom, and by whom? Who gets someone else's good done to them? In *Data Feminism*, we talk about these kinds of questions as "who" questions. These are questions that we have to ask when we say "data science for good." There is a lot to unpack when we make statements about what is "good." That is why, in the book, we explore how good is usually defined by the dominant social group.

In terms of barriers, we have not yet really interrogated and reconciled who's behind these technologies, who is on their receiving end, and what outcomes they want. Data and AI are tools that require a fairly high amount of expertise to mobilize, and a lot of resources to make. It costs a lot of money to collect, store, and maintain the data and employ the staff who know how to use that data, particularly when this happens at scale for a global platform. What has happened is that the "who" questions have ended up being answered by default, according to the current way that the political economy is organized. This means that it is corporate actors, generally, who are answering these questions.

So "good" in a lot of these cases just means what is good for the company, which means focusing all of those resources on extracting the most profit possible or, if there's any kind of social component, telling heart-warming stories that function as PR for corporations. I see what is good for corporations as being fundamentally in tension with what is good for people and communities and for justice.

This is why we need a feminist perspective. Now, there are many feminisms and not all feminisms are compatible with each other. Lauren and I, in *Data Feminism*, draw specifically from intersectional feminism.[1] This is a feminist framework that comes out of US Black feminisms. Kimberlé Crenshaw created the term "intersectionality," but there were many precursors to her work.[2] For example, the Combahee River Collective, a Black feminist lesbian socialist organization active in Boston from 1974 to 1980.[3]

There are scholars like Vivian May and Brittney Cooper who have traced the history of intersectionality as a concept back to the nineteenth century.[4]

An intersectional feminist approach says that there is really no way, when we think about social inequality, that you can only look at one dimension of social inequality—like sex or gender—as the only vector of oppression. Specifically, Crenshaw was talking about the experiences of Black women who sit at this intersection of combined racism and sexism, and the unique, nonlinear way in which sexism and racism combine to shape their life experiences and possibilities.[5]

Intersectionality is a very powerful justice framework, and has been developed further as social theory.[6,7] It says that a narrow focus on one dimension of oppression is really reductive. It gives us a way to better understand the interlocking nature of structural forces. Intersectional feminism asks us to take these structures into account as we make these differentials of power visible. It arises from considering the experiences of Black women. At the same time, the Combahee River Collective said that if Black women were free, then all of us would be free, because it would mean the destruction of all forms of domination and oppression.[8] This is one of the things that, for me, is very powerful about intersectionality—it starts with a unique and grounded specificity and then can be applied in other contexts, and I think that is its power.

In *Data Feminism* we propose seven principles. We developed the book by looking at feminist literature from across a variety of different fields. We always had intersectionality and Patricia Hill Collins's "matrix of domination" as the undergirding theories of power that underlie our work.[9] And then once we had looked across more feminist scholarship and activism, we came up with seven principles that, for us, really encapsulate the most important aspects of feminism as they relate to data science, while challenging the practice of doing data science itself.

So those are things like Examine Power, Challenge Power, Rethink Binaries and Hierarchies, Elevate Emotion and Embodiment, and so on. These are distillations of feminist thought that can help us understand how current practices in data science are sometimes subtly—and not subtly—working against doing "good" as feminism would define it. In this case, "good" means working towards justice, equity, and co-liberation.

Fundamentally, *Data Feminism* is responding to the question of why we keep producing racist, sexist, and classist technology. We are trying to back up and examine the root causes, because racist and sexist data and information products are very logical outcomes of a patriarchal and white supremacist society. For example, in the "Examine Power" chapter we talk not only about ways that algorithms and data sets are biased but also less examined issues, like "missing datasets." In Mimi Ọnụọha's, 2016 art project, for example, she sets out to collect a list of what she calls missing datasets: aspects of the world that one might think of as being really socially important, but which nobody collects data about.[10] These include things like maternal mortality statistics at the federal level. Or, for a long time in the United States, we were also not collecting race and ethnicity-specific Covid-19 data.

Ọnụọha's project displays the names of these missing datasets in the form of a filing cabinet with folders inside, which are titled with the subject of the data that are missing. When you open up the folder you discover that there is nothing inside because we have no records about that particular issue. Some of the questions that this project raises are: Why don't these data exist? Why do we have no information? Who is the responsible authority for collecting and stewarding such data and why haven't they invested sufficient resources in it? All too often these are data that have to do with either people that are minoritized or issues that are stigmatized, and so they go underreported.

With *Data Feminism*, we also wanted to make a very specific intervention by showing data and technology people that feminism has so much to offer them as an intellectual tradition. That was one of the great pleasures of the book: looking at all the amazing feminist work has been done in so many different fields, both technical fields as well as in the social sciences, arts, and humanities. We wanted to push back against popular conceptions of what feminism is and who is a feminist. Often the images that people bring to the table when they think about feminists are the product of the powerful backlash against feminism.

We think about how we can use data science to challenge oppression and work toward the liberation of minoritized people, and by extension, all of us. That is unfortunately not the central goal of "good" data science right now. Maybe it will be in the future. But data science as it is currently being taught and utilized in the majority of university departments and corporations is not viewing imbalances in power as a key problem to solve. In fact, there are typically no discussions around structural oppression, and data science is taught in a way that imagines that it is separate from the social and political realm.

Isolation
In fact, there are typically no discussions around structural oppression, and data science is taught in a way that imagines that it is separate from the social and political realm.

We really need a systemic shift, where working with technology always includes thinking about who is building these systems, and who is pushed out from these fields when they result in lucrative tech-bro software platforms. One really disheartening recent example is the firing of Dr. Timnit Gebru at Google over a paper that she was writing about the harmful effects of large natural language processing models.[11] That, to me, demonstrates a huge lack of commitment on the part of the tech industry to truly realize any kind of social good or justice in their products. It says a lot about where the company's allegiances lie.

Fundamentally, corporations are accountable to shareholders and this affects how they are structured and organized. Profit is the shareholders' metric of success. I think that is almost irreconcilable with "good," because profit is always going to be on the side of the status quo and those who already have money and power and do not want to give it up. That is where I see the role of strong government regulation in reining in the profit motive driving tech that is extractive, exploitative, and is exacerbating systemic inequality across the board. One of the more heartening things, despite Dr. Gebru's firing, is that Google employees are unionizing; workers are really taking action from within large tech companies to make change. The path that I see moving us in that direction is one made up of different surges of activism and government regulation—that is, the proactive, not reactive, regulation of these systems.

One maxim that I always come back to is Frederick Douglass' quote: power concedes nothing without a demand. I would not advise that we sit around and wait for companies to make these changes, because for the most part they think they are fine and they are happy with the status quo. Of course, they want more women or people of color to improve their diversity metrics, and they will hire diversity officers and give them no power so that little to no meaningful change happens. So, I am not going to sit around and wait for a major redistribution of power to happen. That is why I am heartened when community activism or internal pressure within the organization becomes strong enough for a company to realize that it cannot abide by a status quo way of operating. There needs to be pressure on people in power to be accountable to different objectives and different communities.

Power
I am heartened when community activism or internal pressure within the organization becomes strong enough for a company to realize that it cannot abide by a status quo way of operating.

We also need to address power in design. My background is in art and design where one is constantly thinking about questions like "for whom is the work accessible and how does it speak to them?" The mode, form, or aesthetics in which you communicate something invites certain people in while excluding others. Highly technical and complex data visualizations that might be very appropriate for an expert scientific audience might, when presented to the general public, make everyone feel stupid—they are going to have a really different effect. It's not going to bring them into the conversation, but actively work to exclude them.

We describe many examples in the book that we call "visceralisations of data," which is actually a term from the artist Kelly Dobson. These include quilts made from data, walking data visualizations, and even the Tanzania Data Lab's Data Zetu Initiative, which culminated in a fantastic fashion show made of data-driven garments.[12,13] These are very creative, embodied ways of working and interacting with data. We show a lot of work by artists and data journalists in the book because they are driving forward new methods of making data accessible to larger and larger publics, not only to expert or narrow professional audiences.

In the book we talk about the projects that leverage data for feminist ends. We call these *counterdata* projects, where they're either collecting or combining data in new ways in order to advocate for specific social changes. You can think about counterdata science as a subset of data activism. For example, we talk about the work of María Salguero, who works in Mexico collecting data about feminicide, gender-related killings. And it turns out there are many individuals and organizations that produce data about feminicide. With relatively few resources and not much institutional infrastructure, data activists are piecing together a data pipeline for how they collect information about feminicide and what they do with the information.[14]

It is not only about producing alternative statistics to government numbers. It also involves taking creative actions with their data, producing art projects, community vigils, large-scale interventions in public space, and more. There's a really interesting way in which data and digital technologies are supporting these kinds of digital feminist practices that then get reinserted into physical spaces. This is a way that data is infrastructuring activists' counter-power practices.

Thus, it is not a foregone conclusion that data are wielded only by the powerful to secure their power. We can—and some of us are already—using data toward community defense, public mobilization, and transformative social justice.

Notes

1. Catherine D'Ignazio and Lauren F. Klein, *Data Feminism* (Cambridge, MA: MIT Press, 2020).
2. Kimberlé Crenshaw, "Mapping the Margins: Intersectionality, Identity Politics, and Violence Against Women of Color," *Stanford Law Review* 43, no. 6 (1991): 1241–99.
3. Combahee River Collective, "The Combahee River Collective Statement," *Home Girls: A Black Feminist Anthology* 1 (1983): 264–74.
4. Jennifer C. Nash, *Black Feminism Reimagined: Life After Intersectionality* (Durham: Duke University Press, 2019).
5. Crenshaw, "Mapping the Margins."
6. Patricia Hill Collins, *Black Feminist Thought: Knowledge, Consciousness, and the Politics of Empowerment* (Milton Park: Routledge, 2002).
7. Patricia Hill Collins, *Intersectionality as Critical Social Theory* (Durham: Duke University Press, 2019).
8. Combahee RiverCollective, "The Combahee River Collective Statement."
9. Collins, *Black Feminist Thought*.
10. Mimi Ọnụọha, "The Library of Missing Datasets," 2016, https://mimionuoha.com/the-library-of-missing-datasets.
11. Emily M. Bender, Timnit Gebru, Angelina McMillan-Majorand, and Shmargaret Shmitchell, "On the Dangers of Stochastic Parrots: Can Language Models Be Too Big?" in *Proceedings of the 2021 ACM Conference on Fairness, Accountability, and Transparency* (2021): 610–23.
12. Elizabeth Borneman and Elizabeth Denise, "Data Visualizations for Pperspective Shifts and Communal Cohesion" (Thesis, Massachusetts Institute of Technology, 2020).
13. Maana Katuli, "Young Artists Use Fashion and Data to Promote Dialog on Sexual Health," *Data Zetu*, January 2, 2019, https://medium.com/data-zetu/young-artists-use-fashion-and-data-to-promote-dialog-on-sexual-health-517429662ec2.
14. Catherine D'Ignazio, Isadora Cruxên, Helena Suárez Val, Angeles Martinez Cuba, Mariel García-Montes, Silvana Fumega, Harini Suresh, and Wonyoung So, "Feminicide and Counterdata Production: Activist Efforts to Monitor and Challenge Gender-Related Violence," *Patterns* 3, no. 7 (2022): 100530.

20

Good Technology Is Free (At Least for a Moment)

Frances Negrón-Muntaner

Eleanor worked with Frances during her PhD on a project of short films, and was quickly taken by her sense of fun and relaxed energy. At the time, Frances realized that the university's Rare Book & Manuscript library only had one Latino collection, and there were few spaces to show visual works by Latinos and other people of color. Frances responded by founding a micro-gallery in a corridor and becoming the founding curator of the Latinos Arts and Activisms collection which preserves and makes available what she calls "archives of possibility." Frances brings her anarchic and joyful outlook to all projects, including the one she discusses in this chapter. She also uses art, filmmaking, curation, and scholarship to shed light on society, politics, and sexuality, particularly in relation to Latinos in films such as AIDS in the Barrio, Brincando el Charco: Portrait of a Puerto Rican, *and* War for Guam.

Let me explain. It was late 2018 and I was working with prop master Walter "Tichín" Santaliz to design a customized Automated Teller Machine (ATM) for the Puerto Rico artivist intervention Valor y Cambio [Value/Valor and Change]. The idea was for the ATM to randomly dispense one of six art currency notes named Personas de Peso Puerto Rico, or pesos for short, ranging in value from 1 to 25. The bills featured people and places that embodied the project's values of creativity, equity, justice, and solidarity. Among them were feminist labor organizer Luisa Capetillo, humanitarian baseball star Roberto Clemente, and the Caño Martín Peña community, which is the only place in Puerto Rico where residents collectively own the land.

To receive the pesos, the participants would respond to three ATM prompts: "What do you value the most or is most important for you, your family, and your community?"; "what changes do you think are needed to support what you value?"; and "tell us a story about a person or group who already does what you value." In exchange for the participant's story, the dispensed bill told its bearer's tale via a QR code on the back that led to a webpage.[1] To complete the exchange, we planned to share the stories of the forty-two organizations and businesses accepting the bills for goods and services during the project's run in February 2019. As printed in the bills, Valor y Cambio's promise was "to tell stories of value" in a manner that is "voluntary and free."

Yet, regardless of how we sketched out the ATM, its cost neared $25,000. I considered raising the amount or charging it. But I felt troubled by both options. Valor y Cambio aimed to provide an experience of a nonextractive, equitable, and ecologically sound economy whose unit of value was the exchange of stories, not the purchase of commodities. We also designed Valor y Cambio to combat the idea that austerity—a punishing policy disproportionately affecting women, Blacks, and low-income communities—was the solution to Puerto Rico's 72-million government debt.[2] Furthermore, if nearly half of Puerto Rico's population lived under the poverty line, and the island's per capita income was $14,000, spending $25,000 on an art object we would only use for less than two weeks was unethical.[3]

So, the ATM had to be free. Tichín and I started looking for a relic to add an inexpensive camera, audio recorder, and bill dispenser. The resulting ATM would be a technology in the etymological sense of "art, skill, craft"[4] and in the contemporary sense of a designed artifact to enhance human capacity and freedom. The ATM would no longer function as a terminal in a financial network. Instead, it would become a technology of transformation to convey that a just economy was possible and "in our hands."

Initially, it was unclear how to procure such a machine. But after multiple calls, we found an ATM maintenance business willing to donate a retired one. Still, the owner's conditions were a bit unnerving. We could not pick up the ATM in his business or home. He instructed us to meet his men in the vacant parking lot of an abandoned Walgreens at night. When I asked Tichín what the donor's name was, he smiled and said: "I don't know."

I feared we could die getting this free machine. As an artist, however, I was even more afraid of the alternative: not to have it. My instinct was the project would fail without the ATM, which once found, we renamed VyC, but most referred to it as "la máquina" (the machine). Though a part of the extractive economy we rejected, the ATM was our star: a familiar object capable of legitimizing the notion that community currencies and other just economy strategies were "real." The new ATM would also be a way to model our method—infrastructure disobedience. It would show that through working creatively and collectively, groups can redirect existing technologies to meet pressing needs.

Of course, repurposing technology was easier said than done. Recruiting a highly skilled engineer proved particularly difficult. So was locating inexpensive parts that worked. Yet, just a few hours before the public test day on February 8, the project's engineer Víctor "Pochi" Maldonado got the ATM to run. Despite limited publicity, people immediately started milling around the machine, and stories began to pour at Deaverdura, a criollo restaurant at Old San Juan. That day, close to a hundred people exchanged their stories for pesos. Over eight nonconsecutive days, more than 1,000 participated.

The VyC's tremendous success confirmed our hypothesis: "la máquina" inspired and afforded our proposal legitimacy. But it went beyond. In addition to affording us creative freedom devoid of debt, the ATM liberated participants in unexpected and transformative ways.

For younger participants, "dialoguing" with the machine allowed them to freely speak their minds outside of adult supervision and symbolize their value to the community. As one teen put it, in contrast to parents and institutions, Valor y Cambio "listened and valued their words"; what young people had to say was so valuable that the machine recorded it. Moreover, the project rewarded their effort and time through a rarely experienced but highly desired freedom: to decide what to do with their money. Many adults, particularly men, also found interacting with the ATM more liberating than speaking to someone, if for different reasons. A number left the booth in tears reflecting on how much a person meant to them or saying something out loud they hadn't before. The ATM acted as a confessional where participants felt free to share ideas and intimate feelings—without dogma or judgment.

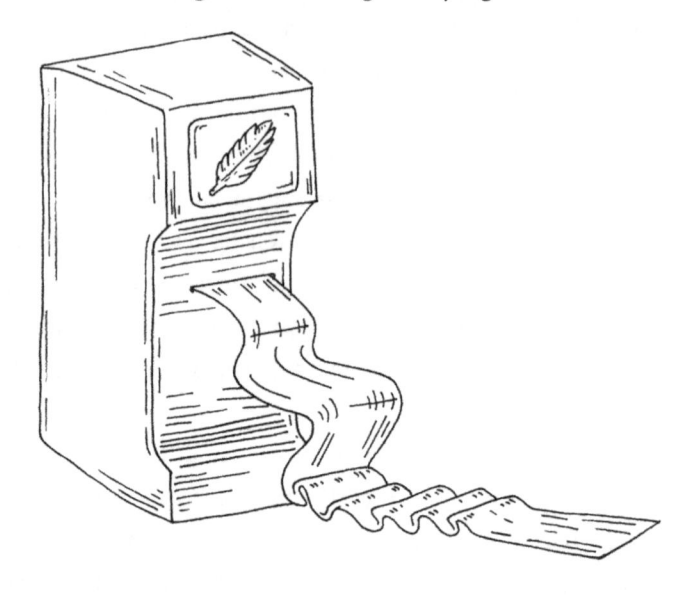

Unbiased Storytelling and Storykeeping
What young people had to say was so valuable that the machine recorded it.

More generally, the experience appeared to not only produce the feeling of personal freedom but also enable different forms of collective liberation. The majority of participants who displayed strong emotion did so when the ATM dispensed a bill whose story deeply resonated with their sense of justice. This emotion was almost always joy, which recalled Thomas Aquinas's eloquent insight that joy is a response to being "united with what we love."[5] I termed this response decolonial joy or the "feeling" that a world free of colonialism and coloniality is possible, that this vision is shared, and that those who share it can bring about change by acting together.[6] The desire to hold on to that emotion similarly explains why most people did not exchange their pesos. They viewed the bills as beautiful art that signified decolonial, feminist, queer, and Black (among other) just futures they did not want to part with or transact.

Decolonial joy is also akin to Baruch Spinoza's concept of joy as a form of resistance that arises as a person actualizes their capacities and "strives to persevere in its own being."[7] In circulating stories of past and present capacity to overcome coloniality, Valor y Cambio challenged the enduring myths of

Puerto Ricans as inherently lazy and inferior and therefore condemned to interminable colonial subjection. Most immediately, Valor y Cambio demonstrated capacity through the ability of a small art initiative led by women to influence a vital conversation that excludes them and by supporting the creation of Puerto Rico's first community currency at the Caño Martín Peña. Named the "Pasos [steps] del Caño Martín Peña," the zone's governing organization dispenses pasos to members whose contributions bring the community a step closer to their collective goals.[8]

The ATM was then good technology for Valor y Cambio. But it was not without glitches. As much as the project's design emphasized communal histories, the ATM's allure was tied to the fetishization of money and machines, in the classic Marxist sense of attributing human qualities to objects while obscuring the inequitable social relations producing them.[9] Furthermore, for some, the fact that the ATM randomly dispensed bills "for free" made the experience seem like a game through which one could magically become rich. From a just economy perspective, the ATM was likewise "bad technology." Marketed as a convenient device to avoid lines at the bank and provide access to money in more locations at all times, the ATM has anti-labor roots. In Europe, banks in the 1960s largely invested in the ATM to curb costs and weaken unions.[10] The device's ubiquity and use of cameras also contributed to normalizing surveillance and monitoring technologies.

In addition, not everyone enjoyed the ATM. When the project relocated to New York, first in the Lower East Side and later in "El Barrio" (East Harlem), Puerto Ricans and other participants of color were occasionally apprehensive. Despite greater fear of crime on the island, more New Yorkers felt unsafe stepping into the enclosure we built to ensure higher-quality recordings. Some asked if we were conducting experiments on the community, a reasonable fear given the long history of medical and other forms of testing on Puerto Ricans. Others were uncomfortable knowing that the ATM recorded them and asked for limited personal information including name, age, and birthplace. This last element of design, meant to help contextualize the responses, reminded participants of the repressive history of the US government toward anti-colonial and other progressive movements. In interacting with the ATM, these participants recalled how US institutions such as the FBI designed and weaponized image technologies to persecute, arrest, and jail activists.

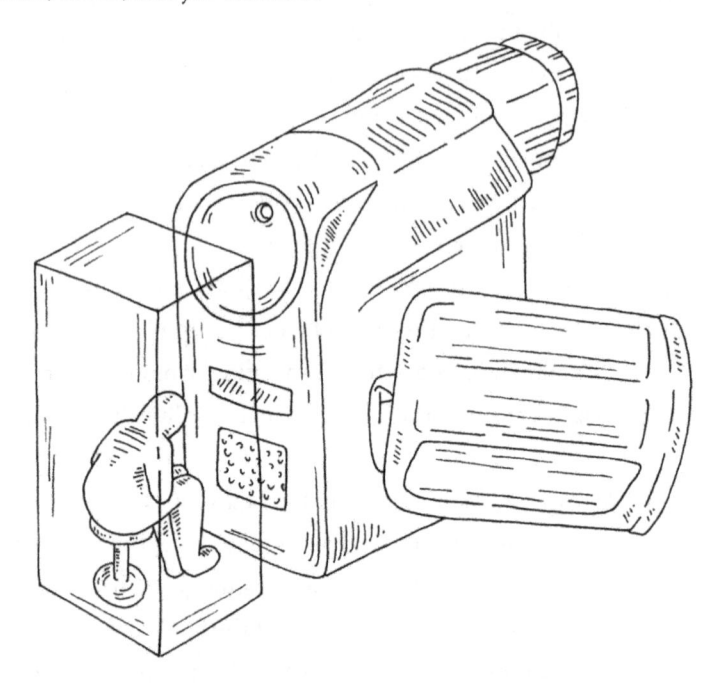

Memories of oppression
In interacting with the ATM, these participants recalled how US institutions such as the FBI designed and weaponized image technologies to persecute, arrest, and jail anti-colonial activists.

Even further, the ATM's power completely failed at times. This was evident in Wall Street, home to the holders of Puerto Rico's debt. While many in Puerto Rico were joyous and in Latino New York cautious, pedestrians who worked in Wall Street were hostile. After we invited them to the ATM, most experienced our prompt, "would you like to share a story about what you value?" as harassment. Once we placed the machine in front of the New York Stock Exchange, a police officer quickly approached and asked us to remove the ATM immediately, fearing the VyC was a bomb. When we stationed the ATM in front of the famous bull statue, a few used it as an armrest and tourists completely ignored it. In this location, the machine was not good or bad technology, nor good or bad art. Instead, la máquina was useless and therefore invisible.

So, what to do when freeing technology crashes? In Valor y Cambio's case, the team decided to stop operating after the New York visit. Not because we finished our work or for lack of invitations to tour but, rather, because we were exhausted. At nearly 400 pounds in weight and precariously constructed, it was physically taxing to keep moving the ATM. Without financial support, we could also no longer sustain a small staff, continue to print bills, or maintain the VyC. The only way to keep the machine going would have been to accept the support of the only sponsors the project ever attracted: commercial banks.

Another option would have been to emphasize the "activist" side of artivism and move more deeply into the political realm. Several of us considered this option during Puerto Rico's "hot" summer of 2019 when one million people—a third of the archipelago's population—took to the streets to demand what many had confided to the ATM earlier: a just, transparent, and noncolonial government dedicated to eliminating racism and violence against women and providing affordable housing, universal health care, and quality education.[11] Yet, this path also had its bugs.

As participants made clear, any connection to actual political organizations or parties would render Valor y Cambio suspect. In Puerto Rico's deeply polarized political landscape, the group's unaffiliated status allowed people to trust us and for the VyC to "work" as a freedom machine. The irony could not be more profound: a project anticipating the protests by nearly six months could lose legitimacy by joining them. In the end, we decided to march individually. To transform Valor y Cambio into a political body would require us to build a different machine.

Yet, while not a perfect technology, the ATM pulled its weight. La máquina helped to assemble people, seed new political possibilities, and generate unexpected concepts and questions. Valor y Cambio's arc also emphasized that humans value machines and other "fetishized" objects for their ability to expand capacity, materialize desire, and free the imagination. In scholar Sónia Silva's terms, "all fetishes reduce our choices and freedom to act as autonomous subjects, which we never are. It is equally true that we act through them, that we produce the world through them, and that we change the world through them."[12] Politics then needs good technology, even if what people mean by good (or free) is context-specific, contested, and provisional—as all things human.

Notes

1. To read more about the project and the bills' stories, see https://www.valorycambio.org/.
2. Ed. Morales, "The Roots of Puerto Rico's Debt Crisis—and Why Austerity Will Not Solve It," *The Nation*, July 8, 2015, https://www.thenation.com/article/archive/the-roots-of-puerto-ricos-debt-crisis-and-why-austerity-will-not-solve-it/.
3. United States Census, https://www.census.gov/quickfacts/PR.
4. "Technology," On Line Etymology Dictionary, https://www.etymonline.com/word/technology.
5. Quoted in M. Volf, "Joy and the Good Life," *ABC Religion and Ethics*, 2016. www.abc.net.au/religion/joy-and-the-good-life/10096486.
6. Frances Negrón-Muntaner, "Decolonial Joy: Theorising from Valor y Cambio," in *Cultures of Equality*, ed. Suzanne Clisby and Mark Johnson (London: Routledge, 2020), 171–94.
7. de Benedictus [Baruch] Spinoza, *The Ethics of Benedict de Spinoza* (Cambridge, MA: Harvard University, 1876), 136.
8. "Inaugura proyecto comunitario de gran valor social en el Caño Martín Peña," *El calce*, October 2, 2019, https://www.elcalce.com/contexto/inaugura-proyecto-comunitario-gran-valor-social-cano-martin-pena/.
9. Karl Marx, "The Fetichism of Commodities and the Secret Thereof," in *Capital: A Critique of Political Economy*, 2005, https://web.stanford.edu/~davies/Symbsys100-Spring0708/Marx-Commodity-Fetishism.pdf.
10. Bernardo Bátiz-Lazo, "A Brief History of the ATM: How Automation Changed Retail Banking, an Object Lesson," *The Atlantic*, March 26, 2015, https://www.theatlantic.com/technology/archive/2015/03/a-brief-history-of-the-atm/388547/.
11. F. Negrón-Muntaner, "Puerto Rico Remade," *Dissent Magazine*, August 7, 2019, www.dissentmagazine.org/online_articles/puerto-rico-remade.
12. Sónia Silva, "Reifcation and Fetishism: Processes of Transformation," *Theory, Culture & Society* 3, issue 1 (January 28, 2013), https://journals.sagepub.com/doi/abs/10.1177/0263276412452892.

21

Good Technology Subverts Militarism

Katherine Chandler

Kerry first met Kate when she gave a brilliant presentation at a conference they were both attending, during which Kate read aloud a speculative fiction story that offered a feminist rethinking of drone technologies. She was blown away by Kate's ability to tell compelling stories about complex topics. Kate brings her aptitude for storytelling and her commitment to imagining different kinds of technological worlds to her essay. Across her various projects, Kate looks at how militarism is embedded in all sorts of everyday technologies, from email to PowerPoint. She also uses art, like storytelling, to challenge the histories of power and control that shape technologies like drones, and to draw attention to how drones are currently being deployed for purposes as varied as humanitarian aid and wildlife management on the African continent. Kate is also a brilliant teacher, creating classroom spaces that challenge top-down teaching and encourage students to become radical critics in their own right. Every time we chat to Kate, we learn something unexpected and new, so we feel jealous of the students who get the chance to learn from her on a day-to-day basis!

I recently met up with a colleague who shared with me a common sentiment: "technology is fantastic." Look, for example, at the advances made by the internet, transport, and communication. While this understanding is widely shared and, often, taken for granted, I think the claim is misplaced. Whether a technology is good or bad depends on context. This means that technologies should be judged through the social, economic, political, and cultural relations that they are both created by and produce.[1] Such an understanding undoes a simple binary between good and bad. It also calls on us to interrogate the military origins of many technological systems and reflect on the ways violence and division are embedded in technology's development and use.

I contribute to a branch of feminist scholarship studying everyday militarisms. We study how war is embedded in everyday experience and investigate how, across temporalities, scales, and histories, militarized conditions are made ordinary. Our research starts from situated and embodied experiences and troubles taken-for-granted assumptions about the state and subject. Militarism is not a narrow field of study defined by military history. Instead, we seek to understand the significance of the military in shaping identities, technologies, and territories and observe its effects in shaping both material and affective experiences.[2] One starting point is the writing of feminist philosopher of science Donna Haraway. Her "Cyborg Manifesto" articulates how gender relations are embedded in mechanical systems, as well as their connection to the military-industrial complex.[3] Haraway's manifesto helped me to see how the category of technology can serve as a critical lens to address the interconnections between identity categories, like race, gender and sexuality, and global divides. Her essay also historicizes current debates on AI and other ostensibly new technologies.[4]

My book *Unmanning: How Humans, Machines and Media Perform Drone Warfare* studies how experiments with unmanned aircraft not only led to contemporary targeted killings by the US military but also tie the aircraft to the development of domestic television in the United States and the normalization of Cold War surveillance as national protection.[5] Watching became a new form of power both in the air and in the household.

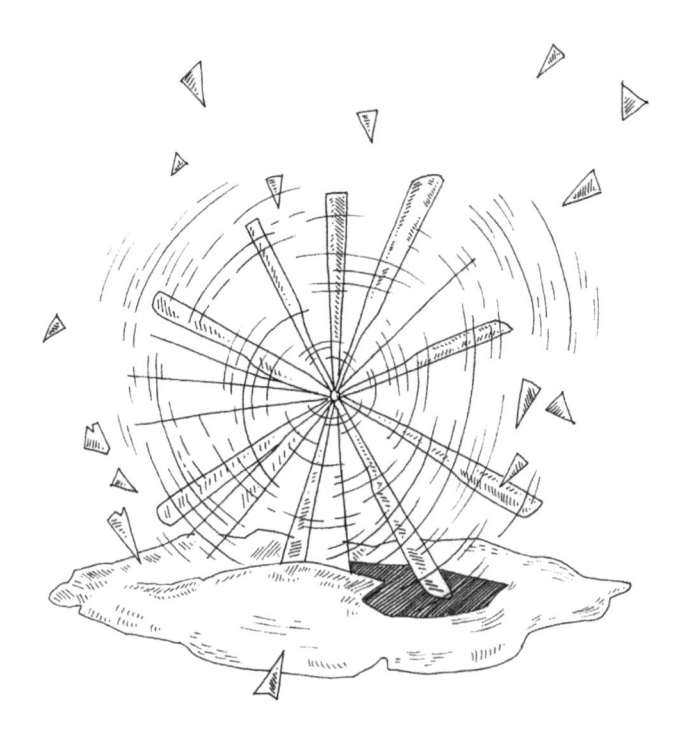

Watching
Watching became a new form of power both in the air and in the household.

I interrogate the concept of unmanning and argue it is a contradiction. What is drone-like is instead made by social, economic, and political relationships and tied to colonial and racial stereotypes. The act of defining what is not human reveals the assumptions that underlie the "human." The name drone, for example, was associated with insect-like control; yet, it was not the inhuman qualities of the drone that the engineers drew on to name remote-controlled aircraft but their ability to be controlled. Countless crashes and failed flights suggest the fiction of the term. This tension between what is in control and what is out of control is important, especially against the common understanding of technology as a tool. When we think of technology as a tool, it is understood as an instrument applied to something else. Yet, as I point out in my analysis, the very concept of control, itself a political, economic, and social idea, is negotiated through the development of technologies, like the drone. The drone is not merely a tool but instead changes the entire context of war and managing territory. Moreover, control also does not always work out as expected, reproducing violence and division both in success and failure.[6]

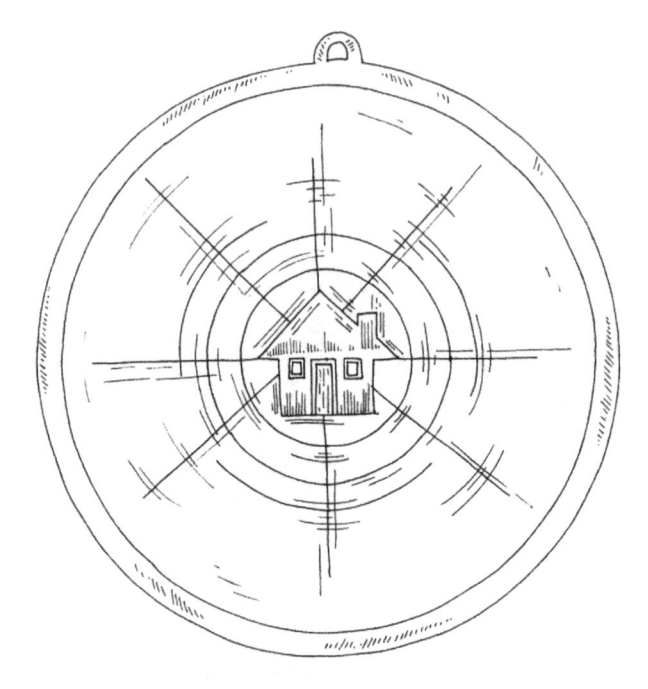

Control
Control also does not always work out as expected, reproducing violence and division both in success and failure.

In my writing, I analyze how a nonhuman counterpart to human action fits with gender, racial, and colonial hierarchies and study how they play out in automated warfare. We can see these ideas in the experimental use of drone aircraft during the Second World War. US soldiers referred to the project as the American kamikaze, which incorporated components of early television. Vladimir Zworykin, an engineer at the Radio Corporation of America (RCA), was a key proponent of the project. "Kamikaze" is a term that was appropriated by the US military to stereotype and dehumanize Japanese pilots. Zworykin describes a television-guided drone he conceptualized as their "humane" counterpart. Here, the idea of remote war simultaneously fits with a racialized idea of the enemy and sacrifice to the state. Against the rise of the so-called mechanical war, a white male subject haunts the drone, shaping global politics under the guise of technological advance. Yet, these drones were also seen as a failure and the experiment was canceled in 1944. Significantly, the leftover parts of the drone aircraft became an integral part of domestic televisions in the United States during the 1950s.[7] After the project's cancellation, the image orthicon developed for the television-guided weapon became the basis of RCA's television set. Industry insiders referred to the image orthicon as an "immy," and the feminized version of the name became the Emmy, one of the most significant awards for American and international television.[8]

Today, some political analysts describe the development of autonomous weapons as an "AI arms race," which typically pits the United States against China. This discussion is usually separate from critiques of AI that point out how algorithms can reproduce and exacerbate racial and gender stereotypes. In my current writing on military AI, I aim to bring these conversations together. I also want to emphasize the significance of failure and unintended consequences in thinking about how new military technologies will be used. My thinking on military AI is informed by analyses of how cybernetics had already shaped and been shaped by the military during the Cold War. Historian of science Peter Galison looked at how Norbert Wiener's theories tied to the automation of anti-aircraft systems during the Second World War, while Paul Edwards theorized how the discourse of a closed world connected the military to early AI research.[9] Other authors, including Lorraine Daston and Nathan Esmenger, have emphasized how gender and sexuality shaped early understandings of AI, as well as the ways computation is tied to gender.[10] Together, these scholars suggest we treat AI within social, political, and economic contexts, not just as a new development. Excavating how AI has already been shaped by the military reveals the limits of some of the current discourse.

One way to think about the connections between the military and AI is through Silicon Valley itself. Before the region was associated with the tech industry, it was known for the military. Both military bases and military industry played an outsized role in the history of the region and initially, early computers received substantial military funding.[11] This legacy not only impacts the development of technology but also shapes the local environment. Santa Clara County, where Silicon Valley is located, also has the highest concentration of Superfund sites in the United States, a designation given to locations with high levels of environmental contamination by the US

Environmental Protection Agency.[12] Technological transformation cannot be disentangled from the toxic chemicals used to make computer chips and semiconductors in the region from the 1960s–1980s. I point to this legacy to think about the connections between digital and physical environments, as well as to alert us to the economic incentives that drive military and technology.

The Costs of War project at the Watson Institute at Brown University calculates that the United States has spent $14 trillion on defense spending in Afghanistan since 2001. Of this, one-half to one-third of all the money spent went to private contractors and five major defense industry corporations received one-third to one-quarter of this funding.[13] The war in Ukraine has served as a catalyst for funding "high-tech" warfare. *The Economist* reported that spending on American aerospace and defense startups tripled between 2019 and 2021, reaching $12 billion worldwide.[14] Currently, the US military budget has earmarked $6 billion for military applications, and AI Tech industry leaders, like Eric Schmidt, former Google CEO, have bolstered these investments, arguing the United States has a "moral'" imperative to develop AI weapons.[15]

Everyday militarism would ask us to think about a different set of questions regarding the "AI arms race." Who is the target of these technologies? How do they perpetuate global inequalities? And can there be another framework other than continuous war to shape the development of AI? In thinking about these themes, I've found it helpful to turn to the work of gender, peace, and security advocates. Feminist activists have a long history of protesting war and violence across the globe. These include, for example, Women Strike for Peace in the United States and the Mothers of the Plaza Mayo in Argentina. I think we can look to these histories—without essentializing what a woman is or overlooking categories like nation, race, class, and ethnicity that prevent solidarity among women—to address military applications of AI that draw out the 'human' that is the backdrop of such systems. Technology, as such, may provide the means to re-examine existing inequalities, global problems, and local challenges. In this way, technology is a critical lens to think about how contemporary relationships might be dissected and transformed. It asks us to consider how we might create relations that are more equitable, more just, and allow us to be the kinds of people that we want to be, as well as better understand our connection to others.

Such a framework might lead to a different set of applications for AI and problems for computer engineers, politicians, investors, and the people who use and work with it, as well as the people they intend to represent. For example, I might imagine a process that would be designed not to turn people into targets but represent them as subjects. It could also mean imagining technology not as a race at all. This would mean changing the language we use to describe innovation, which potentially wouldn't even use the word innovation at all. Rather, we might think about technological processes as engaged with the forms of connection that we want to have in the globe and work to slowly incorporate these ideals into the systems we build. This means not just changing how AI is applied, but also how it is conceived. It also means that we rethink who has stakes in the development of systems like machine learning and other technologies designed to replicate human processes.

By re-visioning technology, we might address the ways violence is embedded in its development and use. We need to unpack how competition and conflict are understood as the basis of technological developments and think of alternatives. Different frameworks for thinking about what technology is, especially in the context of war and economic development, might suggest other avenues for research and investment. These perspectives, moreover, might come as positions and perspectives that are just not normally included in tech and policy conversations. In tandem, we need to think about how money is spent on AI and who drives these decisions. One example is a "AI Decolonial Manyfesto," a provocation about AI written by technologists and human rights advocates who aim to challenge the Western-centric bias of AI.[16] The "manyfesto" rejects a singular narrative for AI defined by masculinity, whiteness, and wealth. Instead, it argues that AI should be defined by communities in ways that "reshape reality in their terms."[17] Technologies, as such, must incorporate multiplicity to advance an agenda that prioritizes dignity over efficiency.

A more expansive, diverse, and heterogeneous approach to AI suggests a different future. Rather than producing an apocalyptic machine-led world, interdependencies between humans and technologies could lead us to refashion global relationships in ways that highlight connections and redress exploitation and inequalities. Part and parcel of this work is promoting systems that foreground collaboration and nonviolence. It would also mean creating meaningful limits to military applications of AI, including, for example, a ban on using the technologies to target people. This would also call on us to recognize a much broader range of expertise in studying and regulating new technologies. Finally, an alternative agenda would expand the research and development of sociotechnical systems that envision social justice, human dignity and the repair of inequalities as their outcome. Rather than everyday militarism, technology might instead be tied to social, political, and economic conditions that produce cooperation and equality.

Notes

1 This argument is indebted to decades of scholarship in the field of science and technology studies. See for example Bruno Latour, "Technology Is Society Made Durable," *The Sociological Review* 38, suppl. 1 (1990): 103–31; Lucy Suchman, *Human-Machine Configurations: Plans and Situated Actions* (Cambridge: Cambridge University Press, 2006); Ruha Benjamin, *Race After Technology* (Cambridge: Polity Press, 2019).

2 Caren Kaplan, Gabi Kirk, and Tess Lea, "Everyday Militarisms: Hidden in Plain Sight/Site," *Society and Space* (2020), https://www.societyandspace.org/articles/editors-letter-everyday-militarisms-hidden-in-plain-sight-site (accessed May 4, 2023).

3 Donna Haraway, "A Cyborg Manifesto: Science, Technology, and Socialist-Feminism in the Late Twentieth Century," in *Simians, Cyborgs, and Women: The Reinvention of Nature*, ed. Donna Haraway (New York: Routledge, 1991), 149–81.

4 Haraway, "A Cyborg Manifesto."

5 Katherine Chandler, *Unmanning: How Humans, Machines, and Media Perform Drone Warfare* (New Brunswick: Rutgers University Press, 2020).

6 Chandler, *Unmanning*.

7 Chandler, *Unmanning*, 37–59.

8 Tim Appelo, "Why it's Called an Emmy," *Hollywood Reporter*, August 16, 2011, https://www.hollywoodreporter.com/tv/tv-news/how-emmy-award-got-name-223077/ (accessed May 4, 2023).

9 Peter Galison, "The Ontology of the Enemy: Norbert Wiener and the Cybernetic Vision," *Critical Inquiry* 21, no. 1 (October 1994): 228–66; Paul Edwards, *The Closed*

World: Computers and the Politics of Discourse in Cold War America (Cambridge, MA: The MIT Press, 1997).

10   Lorraine Daston, "Enlightenment Calculations," *Critical Inquiry* 21, no. 1 (1994): 182–202; Nathan Ensmenger, *The Computer Boys Take Over: Computers, Programmers, and the Politics of Technical Expertise* (Cambridge, MA: The MIT Press, 2010).

11   Lindsey Dillon, "War's Remains: Slow Violence and the Urbanization of Military Bases in California," *Environmental Justice* 8, no. 1 (2015): 1–5.

12   Evelyn Nieves, "The Superfund Sites of Silicon Valley," *The New York Times*, March 26, 2018, https://www.nytimes.com/2018/03/26/lens/the-superfund-sites-of-silicon-valley.html (accessed May 4, 2023).

13   William Hartung, "Profits of War: Corporate Beneficiaries of the Post-9/11 Pentagon Spending Surge," *Costs of War*, Watson Institute for International and Public Affairs, September 13, 2021, https://watson.brown.edu/costsofwar/papers/2021/ProfitsOfWar (accessed May 4, 2023).

14   "Can Tech Reshape the Pentagon?" *The Economist*, August 8, 2022, https://www.economist.com/business/2022/08/08/can-tech-reshape-the-pentagon (accessed May 4, 2023).

15   Eric Schmidt et al., *Final Report: National Security Commission on Artificial Intelligence (AI)*, National Security Commission on Artificial Intelligence, March 5, 2021, https://www.nscai.gov/2021-final-report/ (accessed May 4, 2023).

16   Aarathi Krishnan et al., "AI Decolonial Manyfesto," n.d., https://manyfesto.ai/ (accessed May 4, 2023).

17   Krishnan et al., "AI Decolonial Manyfesto."

22

Good Technology Is a Fantasy

Jack Halberstam

Jack is one of the most prominent figures in gender studies and queer theory. His writing is both radical and gentle, realistic and ambitious, approachable and academically rigorous. He's known for using kids animated movies to think about queerness as wandering, meandering, forgetting, and generally not living up to patriarchal ways of living, his call to embrace "the wildness," his "Gaga feminism," and his avoidance of binary thinking, even when it comes to trans* identities. At the time we interviewed Jack we were very involved with the idea of "queering" technology, and kept insisting on the question. Jack kindly but firmly communicated to us that such a queering was unlikely, and that—certainly in the case of social media—we should just Get Off ("in all senses of the phrase").

I like the phrase *The Good Robot*, because it is such a fantasy from an earlier moment in technological innovation when there was an uncritical sense that humans would invent a robot world that would help us automate labor. These machines would take some of the bite out of all the things that humans do not like doing. Of course, that has not really come to pass. I think the questions about technology now are far less interested in a moral realm of good and bad, and much more into the crisis of ongoing environmental decline. Good technologies now, I think, really need to refer to definitions of technology that are oriented toward solid environmental practices on the one hand, and, on the other, are in keeping with a vision of social—I don't want to say progress—betterment perhaps.

After all, technology can mean anything from a knife or fork to new forms of digital connectivity. So "good technology" is too capacious a term. Any technology could be both good or bad. Our metrics have to fall out of the good and bad dichotomy and instead address how we want to rethink technology in an era defined by a global pandemic; an era in which technology has not succeeded, for all its promise and potential, in helping humans clean up the environment, in improving relations between people, and in reducing social inequality. In my view, the only time technology is good at this point is when it is used as a platform for social justice work.

I am not as hopeful now as I was thirty years ago about the promises of technology. I think that we are all so tethered to the machine that the idea that it is going to work in our favor is a little bit naive at this point. Especially after the pandemic I think we all are interested in "in real life" things (IRL); we would like to be back in physical spaces with other bodies that aren't mediated by screens. We were in a very long pause for a world that is spinning so fast, and it should have given us time to rethink our relationships to technology even as we became more dependent on them during the lockdowns, separations, and social distancing. I think that the opposite, however, is probably true. We have become so reliant on machines that we cannot break from them.

The way that we understand technology has to take into account race and gender, because in the past forty years, certainly since internet culture took over, we've seen an exponential growth in the way in which technology saturates human life. For that reason, if societal divisions between male and female, passive, and active, nature and culture, persist through these technologies, which of course they do, then there is an increasingly unlikely chance that we will ever shake free of those foundations. The more we become thoroughly scripted by our machines, the less likely we are to shake free of binary orientations to the world.

After all, there are technologies that sediment the nature-culture binary that even come in the form of pencils ("oh here, little girls, you can have these pink pencils with tassels and here, little boys, you can have retractable lead pencils"). The problem is that the gender binary is already built into science and technology's way of looking at the world. People often look around their changing culture and say, wow, gender has changed so much in the last ten years, we have even reached a transgender "tipping point" where trans* are now included in and supported by society. It seems as if real progress has been made, until you realize that trans* people are just a new niche market for neoliberal capitalism. So, the emergence of a very strong and vocal trans* community has not completely changed how we see gender. Now that algorithms also channel the gender binary, it cannot be resisted through simple technological fixes. Those social inequities have to be resolved in many places at once: politically, socially, psychologically, structurally, and technologically.

This is a key preoccupation of feminist thinking about technology. Feminist methodologies, for the most part, had to nod to Haraway's early work in order to interrupt the men-only lovefest that dominates the technology industry in Euro-American contexts. Queer and feminist methodologies pay much more attention to the uses of technology, as opposed to just the virtuosic invention of things, and the ways that ideas about the body, social relations, and gendered behavior simply get transferred from society into new technologies.

Feminist and queer technologies, therefore, cannot merely be an add-on or afterthought, but must be a way of thinking about how to improve technology from the ground up. The only way for new technologies to bear any relevance to a rapidly changing world is if the foundational assumptions that they harbor—in relation to gender—can shift and develop. Take, for example, the case of automated gender recognition technologies, which claim to be able to identify a person's gender by looking at their face. Automated gender recognition does not account for the massive social changes in how we have decided to define gender over the last few decades. Gender has changed rapidly in our society with new visibilities of various kinds of trans* people, and with increasing numbers of young people identifying as either trans* or nonbinary. And yet, when you go through a scanner at the airport, or you look into a machine that's scanning your face using recognition software, that machine still operates using a binary recognition mode using the building blocks of zero and one. Because of this, the question remains as to whether we can recognize multiple genders and whether we can use queer and feminist knowledge to question how these technologies are being used in the first place.

Why, when you go through a body scanner at the airport are different bodies represented with pink- or blue-colored buttons? As somebody who is ambiguously gendered, every time I go through that scanner I am in a no man's land, where the machine constantly finds inconsistencies in my bodily presentation. First, the last three times I have gone through the body scanner, the male and female-designated Transportation Security Administration workers have been unsure as to who is to pat me down. Second, they always say there is a problem in the crotch area, and we're going to have to pat you down. We are in an era in which a machine that is supposed to scan the body to detect concealed weapons is actually policing non-normative gender presentation and unfairly targeting and racially profiling certain individuals. We do not, therefore, merely seek to incorporate queer and feminist ideas into existing technology but to transform a technology from the ground up by questioning its foundational assumptions.

We also have to ask what the technology is for and whether we as feminists and queer scholars even want to sign on to the massively distributed network of gender recognition devices that has spread across society. Why are we subjected to all of these forms of technological recognition and scanning in the first place? Better scanners at the airport to keep you safe in the plane are not really about keeping you safe, but about shoring up the nation's borders and intensifying a war that's being fought against people of color and people of Middle Eastern origin within the borders of the United States. It's got nothing to do with the border or your safety, and everything to do with Trump building a wall, that triumphant part of his campaign. Precisely because of American and British white supremacy, bodies of color are particularly vulnerable to capture by supposedly neutral forms of technology.

Biometrics can conceal a very active wing of policing. It represents it as a mere security scan: "don't worry about it, you just pass through this, and then we know that you're not going to blow our plane up, or you're not coming into the country for seditious purposes," or whatever it may be. In fact, very big decisions about you have already been made prior to that scan. They are made in relation to much less tangible metrics than the state uses, and they are applied on a regular basis in ways that constantly give white businessmen around the world a pass while catching all kinds of non-normative bodies in webs of surveillance.

To give you a personal example of this, I have—had—something called Global Entry, which was a deep background check that would be carried out on you once so that you can get, in return, a passport that will expedite your passage back and forth across the US border. This year, when my Global Entry renewal came around, my application was denied after five years of having this passport. People are usually denied renewal on the basis of an arrest or felony charge. Neither of those things have happened to me. The only thing I can come up with is that I sometimes am recognized under two names; my passport says Judith, but my public persona is Jack. I have no other way of explaining why a federal department would not give me a card that I have held for five years rather than simply renewing it.

This kind of failure in the system is more pernicious than a mere tech failure. You cannot change technological problems if they are embedded in racist, sexist, and transphobic culture. It is not that we need a better machine. What we need is a different orientation to security and biometric systems of recognition in the first place. Those are the questions that we should be asking rather than being drawn into a debate about better technology.

So, for example, while trans* people are having to jump many hoops to make changes on their driver's licenses and passports to reflect their preferred gender identity, theorists like Dean Spade are asking the bigger questions, like why does the state need to know your gender? Why are we given these two choices? Why must we adhere to those choices? Why does a passport need to reflect your assigned sex at birth? Spade's point is that the violence of gender conformity is in the details, in the administrative structures that manage us rather than simply in one-to-one violence or in moments of gender nonrecognition.

This idea of recognizing bodies is deeply suspicious to me. We do not want a technology that is better at recognizing bodies; we want bodies that are better at evading technological recognition.

Bodies
We do not want a technology that is better at recognising bodies, we want bodies that are better at evading technological recognition.

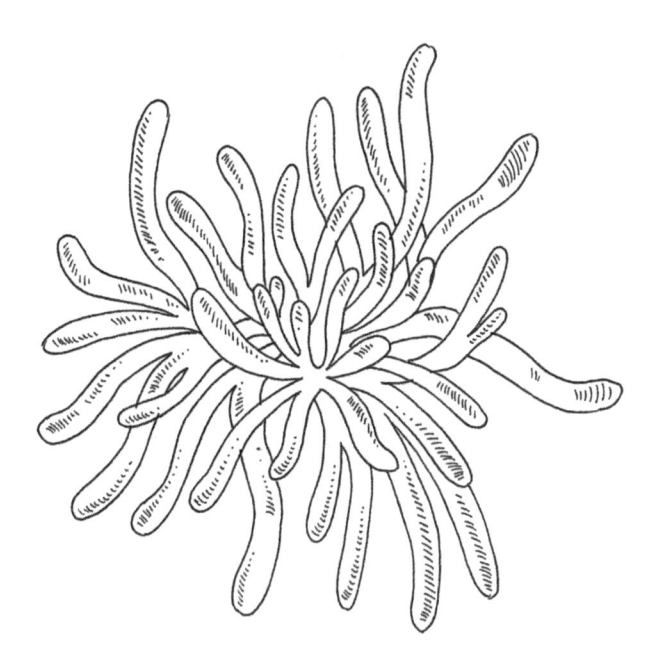

We want to think more in terms of opacity, illegibility, and autonomy in order to evade the technological regimes that seek to capture us. We want different and less regulated ways of making connections that are not constantly being monetized while selling you the idea of staying connected to people. Social media is the best example of how technology is mis-sold. At this point, how people can continue to believe that when they post on Facebook they are just sharing content is beyond me.

Obviously, Facebook, Twitter, and Instagram are incredibly manipulative, pernicious technologies that are collecting information in order to saturate people's worlds with new forms of consumption. The recent acquisition of Twitter by Elon Musk makes it all too clear that the platform is not neutral and has a distinctly right-wing agenda. While most of us know this, we still use these platforms casually and/or obsessively imagining that we are manipulating the platform rather than vice-versa. With the new Musk regime at Twitter, many people are calling it quits. I've written a little manifesto called "Get Off," which advocates for going off-line and for thinking with the pleasures of not being on, not being connected, living separate from these tracking technologies and their addictive content.

Get Off
I've written a little manifesto called 'Get Off', which advocates for going off-line and for thinking with the pleasures of not being on, not being connected, living separate from these tracking technologies and their addictive content.

I advocate for getting off (in every sense of the phrase) not on behalf of a luddite purity but because I believe that the pleasures of assembly have been hijacked by virtual forms of association. I am inspired in my thinking about the assembly by the Argentinian feminist Verónica Gago and her work on "the general strike." For her, this is not simply a strike of workers; it is a strike of domestic laborers who do not get recognized for the work they do, or for homeless people, or for the unemployed who do not enter into the sphere of labor. The general strike is for all of these people who are being marginalized by new forms of governance and technology. I'd like to think of getting off social media, getting off-line, as part of a general strike where we simply withhold our content, our digital labor, our streams of data from all of these voracious and invisible companies that are just soaking up everything that people put out. What if we went on a social media strike?

Just saying.

Contributors

David Adelani is a DeepMind Academic Fellow at University College London, UK.

Meryl Alper is an Associate Professor in the Department of Communication Studies at Northeastern University, UK.

Blaise Agüera y Arcas is a Vice President and Fellow at Google Research.

Neda Atanasoski is a Professor and Chair of the Harriet Tubman Department of Women, Gender and Sexuality Studies at UC Santa Cruz, USA.

Rosi Braidotti is a contemporary continental philosopher, feminist theorist, and Professor Emeritus at Utrecht University, the Netherlands.

Katherine Chandler is an Assistant Professor of Culture and Politics in the School of Foreign Service at Georgetown University, USA.

Anne Anlin Cheng is a Professor of English, and Affiliated Faculty in the Program in American Studies, the Program in Gender and Sexuality Studies, and the Committee on Film Studies, at Princeton University, USA.

Wendy Hui Kyong Chun is Simon Fraser University's Canada 150 Research Chair in New Media in the School of Communication and Director of the Digital Democracies Institute, Canada.

Catherine D'Ignazio is an Associate Professor of Urban Science and Planning in the Department of Urban Studies and Planning at Massachusetts Institute of Technology and Director of the Data + Feminism Lab.

Kanta Dihal is a Lecturer in Science Communication at Imperial College London, and Associate Fellow of the Leverhulme Centre for the Future of Intelligence, University of Cambridge.

Eleanor Drage is a Senior Research Fellow at the Leverhulme Centre for the Future of Intelligence, University of Cambridge.

Jason Edward Lewis is University Research Chair in Computational Media and the Indigenous Future Imaginary and Professor of Computation Arts at Concordia University.

Michele Elam is the William Robertson Coe Professor in the Humanities; Faculty Associate Director, Institute for Human-Centered Artificial Intelligence, and Bass University Fellow in Undergraduate Education at Stanford University, USA.

Priya Goswami is a filmmaker, cofounder of a transnational collective Sahiyo, and cofounder and CEO of the Mumkin app.

N. Katherine Hayles is the Distinguished Professor of English at UCLA and James B. Duke Professor of Literature Emerita at Duke University, USA.

Jack Halberstam is a Professor in the Department of English and Comparative Literature and the Institute for Research on Women, Gender, and Sexuality at Columbia University, USA.

hannah holtzclaw is a Graduate Research Fellow at the Digital Democracies Institute at Simon Fraser University, Canada.

Soraj Hongladarom is a Professor of Philosophy at Chulalongkorn University in Bangkok

Os Keyes is a PhD Candidate at the University of Washington, USA.

Jennifer Lee is the Technology & Liberty Policy Program Director at the American Civil Liberties Union Washington (ACLU-WA), USA.

Kerry McInerney is a Research Fellow at the Leverhulme Centre for the Future of Intelligence, University of Cambridge.

Margaret Mitchell is a Researcher and the Chief Ethics Scientist at Hugging Face.

Frances Negrón-Muntaner is a filmmaker and the Julian Clarence Levi Professor in the Humanities, Department of English and Comparative Literature at The University of Columbia, USA.

Sneha Revanur is the founder and President of Encode Justice and an undergraduate student at Williams College studying Political Economy.

Felicity Amaya Schaeffer is a Professor of the Feminist Studies Department and the Critical Race and Ethnic Studies Department and an Affiliate Faculty in Latin American and Latinx Studies at UC Santa Cruz, USA.

Ranjit Singh is a Senior Researcher at Data & Society.

Index

ableism 7, 111
accessibility 108–13
ACLU, *see* American Civil Liberties Union (ACLU) of Washington
Africanfuturism 165
Afrofuturism 37
ageism 7
Age of Exploration 147
aggregation 101, 102, 105
AGI, *see* artificial general intelligence (AGI)
Ahmed, Sara 52, 129–30
AI, *see* artificial intelligence (AI)
Alexa 126
Alien (Scott) 133
"Along the River of SpaceTime" (LaPensée) 139–40, 144
AlphaGo 19
ALPRs, *see* automated license plate readers (ALPRs)
Amazon 78, 122
American Civil Liberties Union (ACLU) of Washington 71
Anishinaabe scientific knowledge 139
anthropocentric personality 31
anti-racist studies 3
Apple 95, 96
Aquinas, Thomas 182
Argentina
    Mothers of the Plaza Mayo 192
    Ni una menos protests (2015) 169
Argonautica (Rhodius) 160
artificial general intelligence (AGI) 14, 33, 56

artificial intelligence (AI) 6–8, 13, 14, 17, 19, 23–6, 40, 44, 48, 49, 53, 54, 58–62, 67–70, 78, 82–6, 93, 100, 109, 110, 121, 127, 131, 155–8, 160–6, 172
    arms race 191–2
    ethics 4, 45–6, 134, 135, 160, 163
    global knowledge gap in 83
    harms associated with 66
    and humans, relations between 32
    mediated social networks 131
    in military 188, 191–3
    paranoid fantasies about 18
    takeover 163
    Western-centric bias of 193
Asiatic femininity 145–52
Astro Boy 165
Atanasoski, Neda 8
Atari games 19
automated gender recognition technologies 198–9
automated license plate readers (ALPRs) 75
automation 37
Autonomous (Newitz) 31, 166
autonomy 41–2
Azoulay, Ariella 127

Bender, Emily M. 32
Benjamin, Ruha 52, 127, 157
Bennett, Cynthia L. 113
Bennett, Jane 41
Better Images of AI project 160
Biden, Joe 41

Big Pharma   123
biohacking   1, 38
biological determinism   156
Biometrics External Advisory Group   72
Black Lives Matter movement   47
Blade Runner   146
Bloody Chamber, The (Carter)   133
Bostrom, Nick   17, 40
Browne, Simone   76, 127
Buddhism   64, 68–9, 163
"Bulli Bai Deals"   118, 120, 121
Busch, Lawrence   101
Butler, Judith   3, 129

Callous Objects: Designs Against the Homeless (Rosenberger)   73
Cambridge Analytica   120
Capetillo, Luisa   179
capitalism   38, 40, 137, 147
CBP, *see* Customs and Border Protection (CBP)
Cheng, Anne Anlin   8
Cixous, Hélène   133
class inequality   7, 137
Clemente, Roberto   179
climate change   45
Clinton, Hillary   42
Coded Territories (L'Hirondelle)   143
Coding Rights (1990)   120
Coeckelbergh, Mark
    "Human Being@ Risk"   95
cognition, definitions of   28–9
Cold War   191
Colectiva Chamanas of Chiapas   128
Collins, Patricia Hill   7, 173
Combahee River Collective   7, 172, 173
COMPAS   43–4
computational systems   25
Confucianism   163
consciousness   31–2, 42
Cooper, Brittney   172
Costanza-Chock, Sasha   89, 90
Costs of War project (Watson Institute, Brown University)   192
creativity   16

Crenshaw, Kimberlé   7, 163, 172, 173
critical access studies   111
critical race theory   7
Customs and Border Protection (CBP)   72
cyber feminism   37, 41
cybernetics   191
cyborg   41

Dall-E   16–17
Damore, James   51–2
Daoism   163
Dark Matters (Browne)   76
Darwin, Charles   19
Daston, Lorraine   191
data feminism   99
Data Feminism (D'Ignazio and Klein)   6, 8, 78, 171–4
data science   170–5, 177
da Vinci, Leonardo   40
decolonization   125
deepfakes   31
DeepMind   19
Deere, John   95, 96
Deleuze, Gilles   12
D'Emilia, Dani   128
design justice   99
Digital Indigenous Studies (Bernardin)   139
D'Ignazio, Catherine   6, 8, 78, 158, 163, 170–8
disability rights violations   111
disability theory   7, 109–11
discrimination   15, 48, 49, 52, 163, 172
    patterns of   56
    racial   126
    systemic   52, 56, 60
diversity norms   60
Dobson, Kelly   177
Douglass, Frederick   176
Downey, Greg   110
drones   190
due process rights   48
Dunbar-Hester, Christine   97

Elam, Michele 8
electronic benefits transfer (EBT) 113
Ellcessor, Elizabeth 111
empathy 15, 137, 139
Encode Justice 44, 46, 47, 49
enlightenment 23
Enlightenment, the 40
Ensmenger, Nathan 97, 195
environmental degradation 39
equality 5, 7, 58, 59, 194, *see also* inequality
ethnicity 112, 113, 162, 163, 174, 192
Eubanks, Virginia 127
eugenics 14, 126
EVV, *see* mobile electronic visit verification (EVV) apps
Ex Machina (2015) 146, 166

Facebook 120, 122, 135–7, 201
facial recognition 47, 74
Fanon, Franz 129
fantasy 196–202
Faulkner, William 127
female genital cutting/mutilation (FGC/M) 118, 122
feminism 1–2, 7–9, 30, 37, 38, 41, 173, *see also individual entries*
　cyber feminism 37, 41
　data 99
　Gaga 38, 196
　xenofeminism 38
feminist rebellion 169–70
feminist science fiction 37
FGC/M, *see* female genital cutting or mutilation (FGC/M)
FOSS, *see* free and open-source software (FOSS)
Foundation Trilogy (Asimov) 134
Fourth Industrial Revolution 52
Frames of Mind: The Theory of Multiple Intelligences (Gardner) 25
Franklin, Rachel 136
Franklin, Sarah 153–4

free and open-source software (FOSS) 95–6
freemium model 123
free will 30
functionality 66, 68
Fusco, Coco 130

Gaga feminism 38, 196
Gago, Verónica 202
Galison, Peter 191
Galton, Sir Francis 126
GANs, *see* generative antagonistic networks (GANs)
Gebru, Timnit 175, 176
gender 1, 9, 38, 59
　gender-based harassment 119
　gender-based violence 8
　and human rights 8
　identity 166
　injustice 48
　recognition technologies 198–9
　relations 198
　studies 3, 196
generative antagonistic networks (GANs) 31
generosity 102–3
Gen Z 46
Ghost in the Shell 146, 151
Gilroy, Paul 11
Gilson, Erinn 95
Giving Voice (Alper) 108
Glissant, Edouard 11–12
Global Entry 200
Google 86, 120, 122, 175, 176
　GPT-3 (Generative Pretrained Transformer, version 3) 32
　LaMDA (Language Model for Dialogue Applications) 32
grammar 42
Guattari, Felix 12
gun violence 45
Gupta, Apar 120

habits 129
Halberstam, Jack

"Get Off" manifesto   201
Hampton, Lelia Marie   52
Hamraie, Aimi   111
Hansberry, Lorraine
    Les Blancs   154
Haraway, Donna   41, 198
    "Cyborg Manifesto"   188
HCI, *see* Human–Computer
    Interaction (HCI)
health inequality   108
Hickman, Louise   110
historical racism   25
Homo habilus   33
homophobia   7, 109
Homo sapiens   64–5
hooks, bell   7
Hrdy, Sarah   15
Human+   40
human-AI relations   31
Human–Computer Interaction
    (HCI)   21–2
human enhancement   40
humanism   40
    posthumanism   41
    transhumanism   41
human rights   8
Hurricane Maria (2017)   135–6
Huysmann, Joris-Karl   150

ICE, *see* Immigration and Customs
    Enforcement (ICE)
identity politics   11
IFF, *see* Internet Freedom Foundation
    of India (IFF)
IKEA   96
Iliad (Homer)   160
ImageNet   51
Immigration and Customs Enforcement
    (ICE)   72
income inequality   113
Indigenous communities   21
individualism   30
individuation   101–2, 105
industrialization   147
Industrial Revolution   121

inequality   3, 65, 66, 172–3, 192, 194,
    see also equality
    class   137
    health   108
    historic   61
    income   113
    social   25, 41, 108, 110, 173, 197
    structural   108, 171
    systemic   175
injustice   48, 172, *see also* justice
    algorithmic   44–6
    gender   49
Instagram   201
institutional racism   52
intelligence   16–18, 24, 25
    artificia (*see* artificial intelligence (AI))
    superintelligence   40
    task-based   59–60
    technology and   17–18
Internet Freedom Foundation of India
    (IFF)   120
intersectionality   7, 163, 172, 173
intersubjectivity   15

joy   182
justice   15, *see also* injustice
    design   99
    Encode Justice   44, 46, 47, 49
    social   4, 5, 7, 8, 41, 178, 194, 197

Kant, Immanuel   41
Kavanagh, Emma   58
*Kids Across the Spectrums: Growing
    Up Autistic in the Digital Age*
    (Alper)   113
Kite, Suzanne   23
Klara and the Sun (Ishiguro)   32
Klein, Lauren   6, 8, 78, 158, 171–2
Krishnan, Aarathi
    "AI Decolonial Manyfesto"   193

Language Model for Dialogue
    Applications (LaMDA)   32
Large Language Models (LLMs)   58
Law, John   95

Lee, Jen   163
Lemoine, Blake   32
liberal individualism   42
Liezi (Yukou)   160
Litchfield, Chelsea   58
LLMs, *see* Large Language Models (LLMs)
London, Jack   150
Lorde, Audre   133

machine learning (ML)   24, 25, 27, 126, 127, 131
Machines like Me (McEwan)   32
Maldonado, Victor "Pochi"   181
marginalization   57–8, 60, 64
Margulis, Lynn   30
Marr, Bernard   105
Masakhane   81–8
matrix of domination   173
May, Vivian   172
media accessibility   112–13
Metamorphosis (Braidotti)   37
Metropolis (1927)   37, 166
Microsoft   78, 86
    automated license plate readers (ALPRs)   75
Midjourney   16–17
Midnight Robber (Hopkinson)   166
militarism   187–94
military surveillance   74
Mill, John Stuart   42
Mills, Mara   110
misogyny   1, 55, 56, 109
MIT Media Lab   48
ML, *see* machine learning (ML)
mobile electronic visit verification (EVV) apps   111
moral compass   42
Musk, Elon   38, 40, 41, 134, 201
mutual aid   15
My Health My Data Act of 2023   79

Nakamura, Lisa   137
NASA   40
natural language processing (NLP)   81, 83, 85, 87, 90

New York City, Lantern Laws   76–8
New York Police Department (NYPD)   75
New York Stock Exchange   184
Nicomachean Ethics (Aristotle)   68
NLP, *see* natural language processing (NLP)
Noble, Safiya Umoja   127
#NoMoreCraptions   110
Nussbaum, Martha   41
NYPD, *see* New York Police Department (NYPD)

objectification   147
OCEAN personality model   126, 131
Okorafor, Nnedi
    Binti   166
O'Neil, Cathy   127
Ọnụọha, Mimi   174
oppression   1, 15, 43, 47, 51, 70, 158, 163, 173, 174
    class-based   7
    structural   158, 174
    systemic   114
optimization   13–14
Orientalism   125, 146, 147
ornamentalism   145, 150

paranoid fantasies about AI   18
patriarchy   1, 39, 157, 174, 196
Pearson, Karl   126
Penn, Jonnie   3
personhood   147, 149
Plato   150
Poetics of Relation (Glissant)   11
posthumanism   39, 41
postmodernity   94
Pound, Ezra   150
power   171–8
Poynter, Rikki   110
privilege   15

queer
    theory   3, 7, 196

race/racism   7, 48, 76, 112, 135, 137, 147, 154, 163, 174, 185
   historical   25
   institutional   52
   racial binaries   155
   racial discrimination   126
   racial surveillance   52
   structural   52
   and technology, relationship between   125, 146
Regarding the Pain of Others (Sontag)   137
Relation   11–12
relevance norms   60
religious intolerance   109
Request for Proposal (RFP)   72
RFP, *see* Request for Proposal (RFP)
rhizomes   12
robot apocalypse   163
robotics   37–8, 110, 146, 159
Rosner, Daniela K   96

Said, Edward   146
Salguero, María   177
Sanders, Ruper   151
San Diego, smart city streetlights   77–8
Santaliz, Walter "Tichín"   179, 180
scale   100–106
Schaeffer, Felicity Amaya   8
Schmidt, Eric   192
Scientific Revolution   23
self-awareness   31
self-esteem   46
self-reliance   30
sexism   1, 7, 137, 147, 163, 173
   reduction of   52
   in tech industry   52
sexuality   37
Shew, Ashley   113
Shotwell, Alexis   98
Silva, Sónia   185
situated knowledges   163
Slave Revolts (1712 & 1713)   76
slowness   100–106
Social Darwinism   156

social inequality   25, 41, 108, 110, 173, 197
social justice   4, 5, 7, 8, 40, 178, 194, 197
sociohistorical continuum   52, 53
SpaceX   38
Spade, Dean   200
Spektor, Michelle   100
Spencer, Herbert   19
Spielberg, Steven   161
Spinoza, Baruch   182
Stanford Computational Policy Lab   48
Steinem, Gloria   42
Stelarc   17
Stephenson, Neal   119
stereotypes   56
stigmatization   73, 113, 174
"stochastic parrots"   32
structural inequality   108, 171
structural oppression   174
structural racism   52
Subramanian, Reetika Revathy   117
"Subversion of the Human Aura: A Crisis in Representation" (Hayles)   32
"Sulli Deals"   117–18, 120
superintelligence   40
survival   19
Sustainable Development Goals   86
systemic discrimination   52, 56, 60
systemic inequality   175
systemic oppression   114

tacit knowledge   161
Tanzania Data Lab's Data Zetu Initiative   177
task-based intelligence   59–60
Tech Equity Coalition   78
techno-chauvinism   48
technology
   ethics   3
   feminism and   1, 4
   and gender, relationship between   38
   "othering"   18
   and race, relationship between   125, 146

techno-orientalism   146–8
techno-utopianism   108
Tenen, Dennis   31
Ten Thousand Things: Module and Mass Production in Chinese Art (Ledderose)   16
Terminator, The   161
Thatcher, Margaret   15
TikTok   46, 49, 110
Titchkosky, Tanya   112
transcendental rationality   42
transformative politics   40
transhumanism   41
transphobia   1, 7, 200
Transportation Security Administration   199
tribalism   11
Trump, Donald   41
Turing Test   157–9
Twain, Mark   32
Twitter   110, 201
2001: Space Odyssey (Kubrick)   155–6

United States (US)
    Americans with Disabilities Act   111
    Army   74
    Environmental Protection Agency   192
    FBI   184
    Women Strike for Peace   192
Unmanning: How Humans, Machines and Media Perform Drone Warfare (Chandler)   188

Unthought (Hayles)   28
US, *see* United States (US)
utilitarianism   13

Valor y Cambio (VyC, Value/Valor and Change)   179–86
Varon, Joana   119–20, 123
velocity   101, 104
violence   45, 57, 156, 200
    gender-based   8
    gun   45
    against women   185
Virdi, Jaipreet   110
virtual reality (VR)   136–40
visceralisations of data   177
volume   101
VR, *see* virtual reality (VR)
vulnerability   93–9
VyC, *see* Valor y Cambio (VyC, Value/Valor and Change)

Wajcman, Judy   96–7
WALL-E   161
Wiener, Norbert   191
Wilde, Oscar   150
Wittig, Monique   133
Woolf, Virginia   133

xenofeminism   38
xenophobia   109

YouTube   110

Zuckerberg, Mark   135–8, 156
Zworykin, Vladmir   190